Biggles of the Royal Flying Corps

Biggles of the Royal Flying Corps

by Capt. W. E. Johns

Edited by Piers Williams

Purnell

SBN 361 04179 9

Biggles Learns to Fly revised and published by Brockhampton Press Ltd 1955, now
Hodder & Stoughton Children's Books.
Published 1978 by Purnell Books, Berkshire House, Queen Street,
Maidenhead, Berkshire
Made and printed in Great Britain by Purnell and Sons Limited,
Paulton (Bristol) and London

CONTENTS

"Soft landings—and no dud engines."

R. F. C. toast

BEST OF BIGGLES

Biggles is a fictional character and his adventures were first narrated to entertain young readers but his creator, Captain W. E. Johns, has pointed out that he could have been found in any R.F.C. mess of the day and that his exploits were often based on fact.

Biggles joined the Service as a Second Lieutenant when he was barely seventeen. Two years later he was a Major with the D.S.O., the M.C. and the D.F.C—an ace with thirty-five victories to his credit. He had been almost constantly engaged in aerial warfare, and his rapid promotion indicates the terrible casualty rates of the times.

Captain W. E. Johns was a pilot in the R.F.C. on active service in France from 1916 onwards. Like Biggles, he learnt to fly on a Maurice Farman Shorthorn and was "scared stiff" when he lost himself on his first solo flight. He knew the speed and confusion of a "dogfight" and what it was like to see his comrades killed by his side.

The stories in this collection were all originally published in the nineteen thirties, and some were written in a more adult form than others but all of them are based on firsthand knowledge of the R.F.C.

Piers Williams

First Time Up!

One fine late September morning in the war-stricken year of 1916, a young officer, in the distinctive uniform of the Royal Flying Corps, appeared in the doorway of one of the long, low, narrow wooden huts which, mushroom-like, had sprung up all over England during the previous eighteen months. He paused for a moment to regard a great open expanse that stretched away as far as he could see before him in the thin autumn mist that made everything outside a radius of a few hundred yards seem shadowy and vague.

There was little about him to distinguish him from thousands of others in whose ears the call to arms had not sounded in vain, and who were doing precisely the same thing in various parts of the country. His uniform was still free from the marks of war that would eventually stain it. His Sam Browne belt still squeaked slightly when he moved, like a pair of new boots.

There was nothing remarkable, or even martial, about his physique; on the contrary, he was slim, rather below average height, and delicate-looking. A wisp of fair hair protruded from one side of his rakishly tilted R.F.C. cap; his eyes, now sparkling with pleasurable anticipation, were what is usually called hazel. His features were finely cut, but the squareness of his chin and the firm line of his mouth revealed a certain doggedness, a tendency of purpose, that denied any suggestion of weakness. Only his hands were small and white, and might have been those of a girl.

His youthfulness was apparent. He might have reached the

eighteen years shown on his papers, but his birth certificate, had he produced it at the recruiting office, would have revealed that he would not attain that age for another eleven months. Like many others who had left school to plunge straight into the war, he had conveniently "lost" his birth certificate when applying for enlistment, nearly three months previously.

A heavy, hair-lined leather coat, which looked large enough for a man twice his size, hung stiffly over his left arm. In his right hand he held a flying-helmet, also of leather but lined with fur, a pair of huge gauntlets, with coarse, yellowish hair on the backs, and a pair of goggles.

He started as the silence was shattered by a reverberating roar which rose to a mighty crescendo and then died away to a low splutter. The sound, which he knew was the roar of an aero-engine, although he had never been so close to one before, came from a row of giant structures that loomed dimly through the now-dispersing mist, along one side of the bleak expanse upon which he gazed with eager anticipation. There was little enough to see, yet he had visualized that flat area of sandy soil, set with short, coarse grass, a thousand times during the past two months while he had been at the "ground" school. It was an aerodrome, or, to be more precise, the aerodrome of No. 17 Flying Training School, which was situated near the village of Settling, in Norfolk. The great, darkly looming buildings were the hangars that housed the extraordinary collection of hastily built aeroplanes which at this period of the first Great War were used to teach pupils the art of flying.

A faint smell was borne to his nostrils, a curious aroma that brought a slight flush to his cheeks. It was one common to all aerodromes, a mingling of petrol, oil, dope, and burnt gases, and which, once experienced, was never forgotten.

Figures, all carrying flying-kit, began to emerge from other huts and hurry towards the hangars, where strange-looking vehicles were now being wheeled out on to a strip of concrete that shone whitely along the front of the hangars for their entire length. After a last appraising glance around, the new officer set off at a brisk pace in the direction of the excitement.

A chilly breeze had sprung up; it swept aside the curtain of mist and exposed the white orb of the sun, low in the sky, for it was still very early. Yet it was daylight, and no daylight was wasted at flying schools during the Great War.

He reached the nearest hangar, and then stopped, eyes devouring an extraordinary structure of wood, wire, and canvas that stood in his path. A propeller, set behind two exposed seats, revolved slowly. Beside it stood a tall, thin man in flying-kit; his leather flying-coat, which was filthy beyond description with oil stains, flapped open, exposing an equally dirty tunic, on the breast of which a device in the form of a small pair of wings could just be seen. Under them was a tiny strip of the violet-and-white ribbon of the Military Cross.

To a fully fledged pilot the figure would have been commonplace enough, but the young newcomer regarded him with an awe that amounted almost to worship. He knew that the tall, thin man could fly; not only could he fly, but he had fought other aeroplanes in the sky, as the decoration on his breast proved. At that moment, however, he seemed merely bored, for he yawned mightily as he stared at the aeroplane with no sign of interest. Then, turning suddenly, he saw the newcomer watching him.

"You one of the fellows on the new course?" he asked shortly.

"Er—er—yes, sir," was the startled reply.

"Ever been in the air?"

"No, sir."

"What's your name?"

"Biggleswort h, sir. I'm afraid it's a bit of a mouthful, but that isn't my fault. Most people call me Biggles for short."

A slow smile spread over the face of the instructor.

"Sensible idea," he said. "All right, Biggles, get in."

Biggles started violently. He knew that he had come to the aerodrome to learn to fly, but at the back of his mind he had an idea that there would be some sort of ceremony about it, some preliminary overtures that would slowly lead up to a grand finale in which he would take his place in an aeroplane before the eyes of admiring

"All right, Biggles, get in."

mechanics. And now the instructor had just said "Get in!" as if the aeroplane were a common motor-car. Mechanics were there, it is true, but they were getting on with their work, taking not the slightest notice of the thrilling exploit about to be enacted. Only one, a corporal, was standing near the nose of the machine looking round the sky with a half-vacant expression on his face.

In something like a daze, Biggles donned his flying-kit. It was the first time he had worn it, and he felt that the weight of it would bear him to the ground. Stiffly he approached the machine.

"Look out!"

He sprang back as the shrill warning came faintly to his ears through the thick helmet. The instructor was glaring at him, his face convulsed with rage.

"What are you trying to do?" he roared. "Break my propeller with your head? Come round to the front!"

"Sorry, sir," gasped Biggles, and hurried as fast as his heavy kit would permit to the front of the machine. He raised his foot and clutched at a wire to help himself up.

"Not there, you fool! Take your foot off that wing before you burst the fabric!" shouted the instructor from his seat.

Biggles backed away hastily—too hastily; his foot caught in one of the many wires that ran in all directions. He clutched wildly at the leading edge of the lower 'plane to save himself, but in vain, and the next instant he had measured his length on the ground.

The instructor looked down at him with such withering contempt that Biggles nearly burst into tears. The corporal came to his assistance. "Put your left foot in that hole—now the other one in there—now swing yourself up. That's right!"

To Biggles the cockpit seemed hopelessly inadequate, but he squeezed himself into it somehow and settled down with a sigh of relief. Something struck him smartly on the back of the head, and he jumped violently.

"Strap in," said a hard voice, "and keep your hands and feet off the controls. If you start any nonsense I'll lam you over the back of the skull with this!"

With some difficulty Biggles screwed his head round to see what "this" was. A large iron wrench was thrust under his nose; at the same moment the machine began to move forward, slowly at first, but with ever-increasing speed.

Something like panic seized him, and he struggled wildly to buckle up the cumbrous leather belt that he could see on either side of him. It took him a minute to realize that he was sitting on it. "If he loops the loop or something I'm sunk!" he muttered bitterly, as he fought to pull it from under him. The machine seemed to lurch suddenly, and he grabbed both sides of the cockpit, looking down as he did so. The hangars were just disappearing below.

The next few minutes, which seemed an hour, were a nightmare. The machine rose and fell in a series of sickening movements; every now and then one of the wings would tip up at an alarming angle. He was capable of one thought only: "I shall never fly this thing as long as I live—never. I must have been crazy to think I could."

Woods, fields, and houses passed below in bewildering succession, each looking like its fellow. Had the pilot told him they were over any county in the United Kingdom, he would have believed him.

"We must have gone fifty miles away from the aerodrome," he thought presently; but the nose of the machine tilted down, and he saw the hangars leaping up towards him. For a moment he really did not believe they were the hangars; he thought it was a trick of the imagination. But there was a sudden grinding of wheels, and before he really grasped what was happening, the machine had run to a standstill in exactly the same spot from which it had taken off. He surveyed the apparent miracle with wonderment, making no effort to move.

"Well, how did you like it?" said a voice in his ear.

Biggles clambered awkwardly from his seat and turned to the speaker. The instructor was actually smiling.

"Grand!" he cried enthusiastically. "Top hole."

"Didn't feel sick?"

"Not a bit."

"It's a wonder. It's bumpy enough to make anyone sick; we shall

The machine seemed to lurch suddenly, and he grabbed both sides of the cockpit

have to pack up flying if it doesn't get better. Let's go and mark your time up on the board. Enter up your logbook 'First flight. Air experience five minutes.'"

"Five minutes!" cried Biggles incredulously. "Were we only up five minutes? I thought we were at least half an hour."

The instructor had stopped before a notice-board headed "'A' Flight," below which was a list of names.

"What did you say your name was?" he asked, a frown lining his forehead.

"Bigglesworth, sir."

"What flight are you in?"

"Flight? I don't know, sir."

"You don't know?" snarled the instructor. "Then what the dickens do you mean by wasting my time? What were you loafing about here for? These are 'A' Flight sheds."

Biggles stepped back quickly in his nervousness; his heel struck a chock, and he grabbed wildly at a passing officer to save himself from falling.

"Hi! Not so much of the clutching hand!" growled a voice. "This is a flying ground, not a wrestling school."

"Sorry!" cried Biggles, aghast, detaching himself.

"Your name isn't Bigglesworth, by any chance, is it?" went on the officer, a short, thick-set man with a frightful scar on his face that reached from the corner of one eye to his chin.

"Why, yes, sir," replied Biggles hesitatingly.

"Then what are you doing down here? You're in my flight, and you've kept the class waiting."

"I've been flying, sir," protested Biggles.

"You've been what?"

"He's right!" grumbled the first instructor. "He was down here, so I naturally thought he was one of my fellows. I wish you'd look after your own pupils!"

Biggles waited for no more, but hurried along the tarmac to where a little group of officers—all pupils, judging by their spotless uniforms—stood at the door of a hangar.

"Where have you been?" cried one. "Nerky's been blinding you to all eternity!"

"Nerky?"

"Captain Nerkinson. We call him Nerky because he's as nerky as they make 'em! He's crashed about ten times, so you can't blame him. Look out, here he comes!"

"Well, don't let us waste any more time," began the instructor. "Gather round this machine while I tell you something about it."

The pupils formed a respectful semi-circle round the machine he had indicated.

"This aeroplane," he began, "is called a Maurice Farman Shorthorn, chiefly because it hasn't any horns, short or otherwise. Some people call it a Rumpity. Others call it a birdcage, because of the number of wires it has got. The easiest way to find out if all the wires are in their places is to put a canary between the wings; if the bird gets out, you know there is a wire missing somewhere.

"Always remember that if this machine gets into a spin, it never gets out of it; and if it gets into a dive, the wings are apt to come off. Presently I shall take you up in it, one at a time; if anybody doesn't like it, he has only to say so, and he can transfer to the infantry."

His voice trailed away to a whisper as a faint whistling sound reached their ears. All eyes were staring upwards at a machine that was coming in to land. It was a Rumpity, and it seemed to be descending in short jerks, as if coming down an invisible staircase; the pilot could be seen sitting bolt upright in his seat.

A deep groan burst from the instructor's lips, as if he had been suddenly smitten with a violent pain.

"That's Rafferty, I'll bet my hide!" he muttered. "I thought I'd cured him of that habit. Watch him, everybody, and you'll see the answer to the question why instructors go mad!"

Everybody on the tarmac was watching the machine, Biggles with a curious mixture of fear and fascination. A motor-truck, with a dozen mechanics carrying Pyrene fire-extinguishers hanging on to it, was already moving out on to the aerodrome in anticipation of the crash.

The pilot of the descending machine continued to swoop downwards in a series of short jerks. At the last moment he seemed to realize his danger, and must have pulled the joystick back into his stomach, for the machine reared up like a startled horse and then slid back, tail first, to the ground. There was a terrific crash of breaking woodwork and tearing fabric, and the machine collapsed in a cloud of flying splinters. The pilot shot out of his seat as if propelled by an invisible spring, and rolled over and over along the ground like a shot rabbit. Then, to the utter astonishment of everybody, he rose to his feet and rubbed the back of his head ruefully. A shout of laughter rose into the air from the spectators.

Captain Nerkinson nodded soberly.

"You have just seen a beautiful picture," he said, "of how not to land an aeroplane!"

Landed—but Lost

A week later, a Rumpity landed on the aerodrome, and Captain Nerkinson swung himself to the ground. Biggles, in the front cockpit, was about to follow, but the instructor stopped him.

"You're absolutely O.K.," he said, "except that you are inclined to come in a bit too fast. Don't forget that. Off you go!"

"Off I what?" cried Biggles, refusing to believe his ears.

"You heard me. You're as right as rain—but don't be more than ten minutes."

"I won't—by James I won't, you can bet your life on that!" declared Biggles emphatically. He took a last lingering survey of the aerodrome, as when a swimmer who has climbed up to the high diving-board for the first time looks down. Then, suddenly making up his mind, he thrust the throttle open with a despairing jerk and grabbed at the weird, spectacle-like arrangement that served as a joystick in the Rumpity.

The machine leapt forward and careered wildly in a wide circle towards the distant hedge. For a moment, as the machine started to "swing", Biggles thought he was going to turn a complete circle and charge the hangars; but he kept his head, and straightened it.

The tail lifted, and he eased the joystick back gently. To his surprise the machine lifted as lightly as a feather, but the needle on the air-speed indicator ran back alarmingly. He shoved the joystick forward again with a frantic movement as he realized with a heart-palpitating shock that he had nearly stalled through climbing too quickly. Settling his nose on the horizon and holding the machine on an even keel, he soon began to gather confidence.

A nasty "bump" over the edge of a wood brought his heart into his mouth, and he muttered "Whoa, there!" as if he was talking to a horse. The sound of his own voice increased his confidence, so from time to time he encouraged himself with such comments as "Steady, there! Whoa, my beauty!" and "Easy does it!"

Presently it struck him that it was time he started turning to complete a circuit that would bring him back to the aerodrome. He snatched a swift glance over his left shoulder, but he could not see the hangars. He turned a little farther and looked again. The aerodrome was nowhere in sight. It had disappeared as completely as if the earth had opened and swallowed it up. Perspiration broke out on his brow as he quickened his turn and examined every point of the compass in quick succession; but there was no aerodrome.

It took him another few seconds to realize that this miracle had actually taken place.

"No matter," he muttered. "I've only got to go back the way I came and I can't miss it." In five minutes he was looking down on country that he knew he had never seen before.

His heart fluttered, and his lips turned dry as the full shock of the fact that he was completely lost struck him. Another plane appeared in his range of vision, seeming to drift sideways like a great grasshopper in that curious manner other machines have in the air, and he followed it eagerly. It might not be going to his aerodrome, but that did not matter; any aerodrome would suit him equally well. His toe slipped off the rudder-bar, and he looked down to adjust it.

When he looked up again his machine was in an almost vertical bank; he levelled out from a sickening side-slip, with beads of moisture forming inside his goggles. He pushed them up with a nervous jerk, and looked around for the other machine. It had gone. North, south, east and west he strained his eyes, but in vain. His heart sank, but he spotted a railway line and headed towards it.

"It must be the line that goes to Settling," he thought, and he started to follow it eagerly. He was quite right—it was, but unfortunately he was going in the wrong direction.

After what seemed an eternity of time, a curious phenomenon appeared ahead. It seemed as if the land stopped short, ending abruptly in space, so to speak. He pondered it for a moment, and had just arrived at the conclusion that it was a belt of fog, when something else caught his eye, and he stared at it wonderingly. The shape seemed familiar, but for a moment or two he could not make out what it was. It looked like a ship, but how could a ship float in fog? Other smaller ones came into view, and at last the truth dawned on him. He was looking at the sea. It seemed impossible. As near as he could judge by visualizing the map, the coast was at least forty miles from Settling.

"This is frightful!" he groaned, and turned away from the forbidding spectacle. A blast of air smote him on the cheek, and objects on the ground suddenly grew larger. He clenched his teeth, knowing that he had side-slipped badly on the turn. He snatched a quick glance at the altimeter, and noted that it indicated four hundred feet, whereas a moment before the needle had pointed to the twelve hundred mark.

"Good heavens, this won't do!" he told himself angrily. "What was it Nerky had said? 'Never lose your head!' That was it." He pulled himself together with an effort and looked at his watch. He had been in the air an hour and a half, and Nerky had told him not to be more than ten minutes.

He wondered how much longer his petrol would last, realizing with fresh dismay that he did not know how much petrol had been in the tanks when he started. The light was already failing; presently it would be dark, and what hope would he have then of finding his way? He remembered that he had a map in his pocket, but what use was that if he did not know where he was? He could only find that out by landing and asking somebody.

"It's the only way!" he told himself despairingly. "I might go on drifting round in circles for the rest of my life without finding the aerodrome."

He began to watch for a suitable field on which to land.

He flew for some time before he found one. It was an enormous field, beautifully green, and he headed the machine towards it. At the last moment it struck him that there was something queer about the grass, and he pulled up again with a jerk, realizing that he had nearly landed on a field of turnips.

Another quarter of an hour passed, and another large field presented itself; it looked like stubble, which could do the machine no harm; but he approached it warily. Only when he was quite sure that it was stubble did he pull the throttle back. The sudden silence as the engine died away almost frightened him, and he watched the ground, now seeming to come towards him, longingly.

In the next few seconds of agonizing suspense he hardly knew what he did, and it was with unspeakable relief and surprise that he heard his wheels trundling over solid earth. The machine stopped, and he surveyed the countryside, scarcely able to believe that he was actually on the ground.

"I've landed!" he told himself joyfully. "Landed without breaking anything! How did I do it? Good old aeroplane!" he went on, patting the wooden side of the cockpit. "You must have done it yourself—I didn't. But the thing is, where are we?"

He stood up in the cockpit and looked round. Not a soul was in sight, nor was there any sign of human habitation.

"I would choose the only place in England where there aren't any roads, houses or people!" he thought bitterly. "If I've got to walk to the horizon looking for somebody, it will be pitch dark before I get back. Then I should probably lose myself as well as the aeroplane!" he concluded miserably.

He sprang up as the sound of an aero-engine reached his ears. It was a Rumpity, and what was more, it was coming towards him. It almost looked as if the pilot intended landing in the same field.

"Cheers!" muttered Biggles. "Now I shall soon know where I am!"

He was quite right; he was soon to know.

The Rumpity landed. The pilot jumped to the ground and strode towards him; there seemed to be something curiously familiar about his gait.

He stood up in the cockpit and looked round. Not a soul was in sight

"Can it be?" thought Biggles. "Great jumping fish, it is. Well, I'm dashed!"

Captain Nerkinson, his brows black as a thundercloud, was coming towards him. "What confounded game d'you think you're playing?" he snarled.

"Game?" echoed Biggles, in amazement. "Playing?"

"Yes, game! Who told you you could land outside the aerodrome?"

"I told myself," replied Biggles truthfully. "I wanted to find out where I was. I lost myself, and I knew I had got so far away from the aerodrome that I——"

"Lost! What are you talking about? You've crossed the aerodrome three times during the last hour. I saw you!"

"I crossed the aerodrome?"

"You've just flown straight over it! That's why I chased you."

"Flown over it!" Biggles shut his eyes, and shook his head, shuddering. "Then it can only be a few miles away," he exclaimed.

"A few miles! It's only a few yards, you young fool—just the other side of the hedge!"

Biggles sank down weakly in his seat.

"All right, let's go back," went on the instructor. "Follow close behind, and don't take your eyes off me."

He hurried back to his machine and took off. Biggles followed. The leading machine merely hopped over the hedge and then began to glide down again at once, and Biggles could hardly believe his eyes when the aerodrome loomed up; it did not seem possible that he could have missed seeing those enormous sheds.

He started to glide down in Captain Nerkinson's wake. He seemed to be travelling much faster than the leading machine, for his nose was soon nearly touching its tail. He saw the instructor lean out of his seat and look back at him, white-faced. He seemed to be yelling something.

"He thinks I'm going to ram him," thought Biggles. "And so I shall if he doesn't get out of my way; he ought to know jolly well that I can't stop."

The instructor landed, but he did not stop; instead, he raced madly across the ground towards the far side of the aerodrome, Biggles following close behind.

"I'm not losing you," he declared grimly.

Captain Nerkinson swung round in a wide circle towards the sheds, and then, leaping out of the machine almost before it had stopped, sprinted for safety.

Biggles missed the other machine by inches; indeed, he would probably have crashed into it but for half a dozen mechanics, who, seeing the danger, dashed out and grabbed his wings.

"Are you trying to kill me?" Captain Nerkinson asked him, with deadly calm. He was breathing heavily.

"You said I wasn't to lose you."

"I know I did, but I didn't ask you to ram me, you lunatic!"

The instructor recovered himself, and pointed to the hangar. "Go and enter up your time," he said sadly. "If you stick to the tails of the Huns as closely as you stuck to mine, you should make a skyfighter."

Three days later a little group collected around the notice-board outside the orderly-room.

"What is it?" asked Biggles, trying to reach the board.

"Posting," said somebody.

Biggles pushed his way to the front and ran his eye down the alphabetical list of names until he reached his own, and read:

2 Lieut. Bigglesworth, J., to No. 4 School of Fighting, Frensham.

The posting was dated to take effect from the following day.

He spent the evening hurriedly packing his kit, and, in company with three or four other officers who had been posted to the same aerodrome, caught the night train for his new station.

It was daylight when they arrived the following day, for although the journey to the School of Fighting, which was situated on the Lincolnshire coast, was not a long one, it involved many changes and delays. A tender met them at the station and dropped them with their kits in front of the orderly-room.

Biggles knocked at the door, entered, and saluted.

"Second-Lieutenant Bigglesworth reporting for duty, sir," he said.

An ambulance raced towards the scene, and Biggles turned away, feeling suddenly sick

The adjutant consulted a list. "The mess secretary will fix you up with quarters, Bigglesworth," he said. "Get yourself settled as soon as you can and report to 'A' Flight—Major Maccleston." He nodded, and then went on with his work.

Biggles dumped his kit in the room allotted to him, and then made his way to the sheds, where he was told that Major Maccleston was in the air.

He was not surprised, for the air was full of machines—Avro's, B.E.'s, F.E.'s, Pups, and one or two types he did not recognise. Most of them were circling at the far side of the aerodrome and diving at something on the ground. The distant rattle of machine-guns came to his ears.

Later on he learned that the far side of the aerodrome ran straight down into the sea, a long deserted foreshore, on which old obsolete aeroplanes were placed as targets. Scores of officers stood on the tarmac, singly or in little groups, waiting for their turns to fly.

A Pup taxied out to take off, and he watched it with intense interest, for it was the type that he ultimately hoped to fly. An F.E. was just coming in to land, and he stiffened with horror, knowing that a collision was inevitable.

He saw the gunner in the front seat of the F.E. spring up and cover his face with his arms; then the Pup bored into it from underneath with a dreadful crash of splintering woodwork. For a moment the machines clung together, motionless in mid air; then they broke apart, each spinning into the ground with a terrible noise which, once heard, is never forgotten. A streak of fire ran along the side of one of them, and then a sheet of flame leapt high into the air. An ambulance raced towards the scene, and Biggles turned away, feeling suddenly sick. It was the first real crash he had seen.

A flight-sergeant was watching him grimly. "A nasty one, sir," he said casually, as if he had been watching a football match in which one of the players had fallen. "You'll soon get used to that, though," he went on, noting Biggles' pale face. "We killed seven last week."

Biggles turned away. Flying no longer seemed just a thrilling game; tragedy stalked it too closely. He was glad when an instructor landed, turned out his passenger, and beckoned him to take his place. Biggles took his seat in the cockpit, noting with a thrill that it was fitted with machine-guns.

"We're going to do a little gunnery practice," said the instructor, and took off.

Three days later, Biggles was called to the orderly-room.

"What's up?" he asked a sober-faced officer, who was just leaving.

"Heavy casualties in France," was the reply. "They're shoving everybody out as fast as they can."

Biggles entered and saluted. The adjutant handed him a movement order and a railway warrant.

"A tender will leave the mess at six-forty-five to catch the seven o'clock train," he said. "You will proceed direct to France via Newhaven and Dieppe."

"But I haven't finished my tests yet, sir!" exclaimed Biggles, in surprise.

"Have you got your logbook and training transfer-card?"

Biggles placed them on the desk.

The adjutant filled in the tests which had not been marked up, signed them, and then applied the orderly-room stamp.

"You've passed them now," he said, with a queer smile. "You may put up your 'wings'!"

Biggles saluted, and returned to the aerodrome in a state of suppressed excitement. Two thoughts filled his mind. One was that he was now a fully fledged pilot, entitled to wear the coveted 'wings', and the other that he was going to France.

The fact that he had done less than fifteen hours' flying, dual and solo, did not depress him in the least.

The adjutant handed him a movement order and a railway warrant

Biggles was posted to 169 Squadron near St. Omer, which was equipped with F.E.'s. These were two-seaters, and his observer was the New Zealander, Mark Way. His flight commander was Captain Mapleton or "Mabs".—Ed.

A Daring Stunt

"I'm not going to pretend that I know much about it, but it seems to me that if the Huns are going to mass their squadrons—as apparently they are—we shall have to do the same or else be wiped out." Biggles, having ventured an opinion for the first time since he joined the squadron, glanced up, half-expecting a remark about his inexperience.

"He's right," exclaimed Mabs emphatically. "I've been saying the same thing for the last month. Richthofen, they say, has grouped three squadrons together, including all the best pilots in the German Air Force. And, whether he has or not, we know for a fact that he's sailing up and down the Lines with thirty triplanes tagged on behind him. Who's going to face that bunch? Who's going to take on that little lot, I'd like to know? What chance has an ordinary Line patrol of three planes got if it bumps into that pack?"

"Rot!" snapped Captain Rayner, of C Flight. "The more the merrier! Dive straight into the middle of them, and the formation will go to pieces. It will take them all their time to avoid collision."

"Don't kid yourself!" declared Captain Allen of B Flight. "They've got this game weighed up nicely. They didn't wait for us to bump into them this morning—they bumped into us and we jolly soon knew about it!"

There was silence for a moment, due to the fact that B Flight had lost two machines that very morning through the menace they were discussing.

"I think it's a logical conclusion that if we start sending big patrols of twenty or thirty machines against them they'll start flying in fifties or more. Whatever we do, they will maintain numerical superiority, and at the finish formations will be flying in hundreds. A nice sort of game that will be!" declared Marriot disgustedly.

"Well, it may come to that some day, but if it does I hope I'm not here to see it," observed Allen coldly. "I——"

The ante-room door opened and an orderly appeared. "Major Paynter's compliments, and will all officers please report to the squadron office at once?"

There was a general move towards the door.

The Major was in earnest conversation with Toddy, the Recording Officer, when they arrived, but he broke off and turned to face them as they entered.

"Well, gentlemen," he said, "I've some news for you, though whether you'll regard it as good or bad I don't know. Will all those officers who have had any experience of night-flying please take a pace to the front?"

Mabs, a pilot of B Flight, and a pilot and observer of C Flight stepped forward.

"That's worse than I expected," said the Major. "Never mind; this is the position. Whether we like it or not, Wing have decided to carry out certain operations that can best be done at night. As you know, enemy scout squadrons have been concentrated opposite this sector of the Front, and our machines have neither the performance nor numerical strength of theirs. In these circumstances we are going to try to cripple them on the ground. It is thought that night raids will adversely affect their morale, to say nothing of the damage we may cause on their machines or aerodromes. It's proposed to carry out the first raid on a very big scale; other squadrons will participate and keep the ball rolling all night. In order to put as large a number of machines in the air as possible, this squadron will take part in the raid, which will be on Douai Aerodrome, the headquarters of the Richthofen group.

"You don't imagine for one moment that the Huns will take this night-strafing business lying down, do you?"

"Fortunately, our machines are well adapted for night-flying, so for the next two nights I shall want all officers to put in as much practice in the air as possible. It's up to everyone to make himself proficient in the new conditions. Flares will be put out, and lectures will be arranged, which must be attended by all officers on the station. Has anyone any questions to ask?"

"I take it that the attack will be in the form of a bomb raid, sir?" said Biggles.

"We shall attack with all arms—heavy bombs, Copper bombs, baby incendiaries, and machine-guns. Naturally, it is in our own interest to make a good job of the show; if things go according to plan, we shall meet with less opposition when we resume daylight patrols. That's all."

"Well, that's the answer to the question!" observed Mark brightly, when they were outside.

"What question?"

"The thing we were talking about in the mess when the C.O. sent for us—the big Boche formations. We're going to swipe them on the ground!"

"Well, it may be all right," replied Biggles thoughtfully, "but we could have wiped them out in daylight shows if it comes to that. I'm thinking that there is one thing the staff people may have overlooked."

"What's that?"

"You don't imagine for one moment that the Huns will take this night-strafing business lying down, do you? If I know anything about 'em they'll soon be showing us that it's a game two can play. You mark my words, they'll be over here the next night, handing us doses of our own medicine—in spoonfuls. I hope I'm mistaken, but I reckon things will be getting warmish here presently!"

"Well, the staff won't mind that; they won't be here," observed Mark bitterly. "I must say I don't fancy being archied[1] at night; the flashes look ghastly. I've been told that they are a nice bright orange

[1] Archie: anti-aircraft gun-fire.

“It’s going to be perishing cold if I know anything about it,” he remarked, glancing up at the frosty sky

when they are close to you, and a beautiful dull crimson when they're some distance away."

"We shall soon be able to see for ourselves whether your information is correct," returned Biggles. "As long as they're not pink with blue spots on 'em I don't mind!"

The weather on the night decided for the first raid was all that could be desired, considering the time of the year. There was no wind, and a new moon shone brightly in a clear, frosty, star-spangled sky, against which the hangars loomed as black silhouettes.

By the C.O.'s orders not a light gleamed anywhere, for every step was being taken to prevent information of the impending raid from reaching the enemy through the many spies whose duty it was to report such operations.

An engine roared suddenly in the darkness, and the end machine of a long line that stood in front of the hangars began to waddle, in the ungainly fashion of aeroplanes on the ground, towards the point allocated for the take-off; a dark red, intermittent flame curled back from the exhaust-pipe.

"There goes Mabs," said Biggles, who, with Mark his gunner, was standing by their machine.

The planes were to leave at five-minute intervals, which gave each aircraft a chance to get clear before the next one took off, and so lessened the chances of a collision either on the ground or in the air.

"Marriot goes next, and then McAngus, so we've got a quarter of an hour to wait," went on Biggles. "It's going to be perishing cold if I know anything about it," he remarked, glancing up at the frosty sky. "But there, we can't have it all ways. We shall at least be able to see where we are, and that's a lot better than groping our way in and out of clouds; that's bad enough in the day-time! Hallo! There goes Marriot!"

A second machine taxied out and roared up into the darkness.

"Mabs has got to the Line—look!" said Mark, pointing to a cluster of twinkling yellow lights in the distant sky. "That's archie!"

Lines of pale green balls seemed to be floating lazily upwards.

"Look at the onions," he added, referring to the well-known enemy anti-aircraft device commonly known as flaming onions.

A third machine taxied out and vanished into the gloom.

"Well, there goes McAngus; we'd better see about getting started up," said Biggles tersely.

They climbed into their cockpits, and mechanics ran to their wings and propeller.

"Switch off!"

"Off!"

The engine hissed and gurgled as the big propeller was dragged round to suck the gas into the cylinders.

"Contact!" cried the mechanic.

"Contact!" echoed Biggles.

There was a sharp explosion as the engine came to life; then it settled down to the musical purr peculiar to the Beardmore type.

For a few minutes they sat thus, giving the engine time to warm up; then Biggles opened the throttle a trifle and pointed to his right wing—the signal to the mechanics that he wanted it held in order to slew the machine round to the right. While a machine is on the ground with the engine running all orders are given by signals, for the human voice would be lost in the noise of the engine; even if it was heard, the words might not be distinguished clearly, and an accident result.

With his nose pointing towards the open aerodrome, Biggles waved both hands above his head, the signal to the mechanics to stand clear. The F.E. raced across the aerodrome, and then roared up into the starry night.

He did not waste time climbing for height over the aerodrome, but headed straight for the Lines, climbing as he went. Peering below, he could see the countryside about them almost as plainly as in day-time; here and there the lighted windows of cottages and farms stood out brightly in the darkness; far ahead he could see the track of the three preceding machines by the darting flashes of archie that followed them.

A British searchlight flashed a challenge to him as he passed over it, but Mark was ready, and replied at once with the colour of the night—a Very light that first burnt red and then changed to green. "O.K.—O.K.," flashed the searchlight in the Morse code, and they pursued their way for a time unmolested.

Biggles crouched a little lower in his seat as the first archies began to flash around them. It reached a crescendo as they crossed the Line, augmented by the inevitable flaming onions that rose up vertically from below like white-hot cannon-balls; but the turmoil soon faded away behind them as they sped on through the night over enemy territory, the Beardmore engine roaring sudden defiance. From time to time he peered below to pick up his landmarks, but for the most part he stared straight ahead, eyes probing the gloom for other machines.

The planes, of course, carried no lights, and although chances of collision were remote, with machines of both sides going to and fro all the time, it was an ever-present possibility. In night raids it was usual for the machines taking part to return by a different route, or at a higher altitude to the one taken on the outward journey, and while machines adhered to this arrangement, collision was impossible.

Biggles was, of course, aware of this, but he kept an anxious eye on his line of flight in case an enemy machine had decided to take the same route as himself, but in the opposite direction, or in case Marriot or McAngus had got off their course.

Mark suddenly rose to his feet and pointed with out-stretched finger. Far away, almost on the horizon, it seemed, a shaft of flame had leapt high into the air; the sky glowed redly from the conflagration, and Biggles knew that one of the machines preceding him had either reached its destination and set fire to the hangars, or had itself been shot down in flames.

The fire however, served one good purpose, for it acted as a beacon that would guide them direct to their objective. It continued to blaze fiercely as they approached it, and presently the crew of the F.E. were able to see that it was actually on Douai Aerodrome. It looked like one of the hangars. Keeping on a line that would bring him right over it Biggles throttled back and began gliding down.

Orders had stated that machines should descend as low as five hundred feet, if necessary, to be reasonably sure of hitting the target, but the thrill of the game was in his blood, and he no longer thought of orders. At five hundred feet he shoved the throttle open wide, and, pushing the stick forward, swept down so low that Mark, in the front seat, stared back over his shoulder in amazement.

The instant he opened his throttle an inferno seemed to break loose about the machine. Anti-aircraft guns and even field-guns situated on the edge of the aerodrome spat their hate; machine-guns rattled like castanets, the tracer bullets cutting white pencil lines through the darkness. Out of the corner of his eye Biggles saw March crouch low over his gun and heard it break into its staccato chatter.

He grabbed the bomb-toggle as the first hangar leapt into view, and, steadying the machine until the ridge of the roof appeared at the junction of his fuselage and the leading edge of the lower plane, he jerked it upwards—one, two.

Two 112-pound bombs swung off their racks, and the machine wobbled as it was relieved of their weight. Straight along over the hangars the F.E. roared, while Mark stood up and threw the baby incendiaries overboard.

When they came to the end of the line, Biggles zoomed up in a wide turn and tore out of the vicinity, twisting and turning like a wounded bird. Only when the furious bombardment had died away behind them did he lean over the side of his cockpit and look back at the aerodrome. His heart leapt with satisfaction, for two hangars were blazing furiously, the flames leaping high into the sky and casting a lurid glow on the surrounding landscape.

A body of men was working feverishly to get some aeroplanes out of one of the burning hangars; a machine that had evidently been standing outside when the attack was launched had been blown over on its back; several figures were prone on the ground, and one man was crawling painfully away from the heat of the fire.

Biggles zoomed up in a wide turn and tore out of the vicinity

"Well, that should make things easy for the others; they can't very well miss that little bonfire!" mused Biggles with satisfaction. Shells started bursting again in the air on the far side of the aerodrome, and he knew that Captain Allen, in the leading machine of B Flight, was approaching to carry on the good work.

"If our people are going to keep that up all night, those fellows down there will have nasty tastes in their mouths by the morning!" called Biggles, smiling; but the next instant the smile had given way to a frown of anxiety as a new note crept into the steady drone of the engine.

Looking back over his shoulder his heart missed a beat as he saw a streamer of flame sweeping aft from one of the cylinders. Mark had seen it too, and was staring at him questioningly, his face shining oddly pink in the glow.

Biggles throttled back a trifle and the flame became smaller, but the noise continued and the machine began to vibrate.

"It feels as if they've either blown one of my jampots off or else a bullet has knocked a hole through the water jacket," he yelled. "If it will last for another half-hour, all right! If it doesn't, we're in the soup!"

With the throttle retarded he was creeping along at a little more than stalling speed, so he tried opening it again gently. Instantly a long streamer of fire leapt out of the engine, and the vibration became so bad that it threatened to tear the engine from its bearers. With a nasty sinking feeling in the pit of his stomach he snatched the throttle back to its original position, and shook his head at Mark as the only means he had of telling him that he was unable to overcome the trouble.

The noise increased until it became a rattling jar, as if a tin of nails was being shaken. A violent explosion behind caused him to catch his breath, and he retarded the throttle still farther, with a corresponding loss of speed. He had to tilt his nose down in order to prevent the machine from stalling, and he knew that he was losing height too fast to reach home.

He moistened his lips and stared into the darkness ahead, for it had been arranged that a "lighthouse" should flash a beam at regular intervals to guide the bombers back to their nest. Watching, he saw a glow on the skyline wax and wane, but it was still far away.

He looked at his altimeter; it registered two thousand five hundred feet. Could he do it? He thought not, but he could try.

The rattle behind him and the vibration grew rapidly worse; it became a definite pulsating jolt that threatened to shake the machine to pieces at any moment. But he could see the Lines in the distance now, or rather, the trench system, where the patrols on either side were watching or trying to repair their barbed wire.

Two loud explosions in quick succession and a blinding sheet of flame leapt from the engine and made him throttle right back with frantic haste.

"Well, if we're down, we're down!" he muttered savagely. "But I'm not going to sit up here and be fried to death for anybody; the Huns can shoot us if they like when we're on the ground, and that's better than being roasted like a joint of meat on the spit."

Looking behind him he could see flames from the engine playing on his tail unit, and he knew that if he tried to remain in the air it was only a matter of seconds before the whole thing took fire. He switched off altogether and began gliding down through the darkness, straining his eyes in an effort to see what lay beneath.

In the uncanny silence he could hear the reports of the guns on the ground, and even hear the rattle of machine-gun fire. A searchlight probed the sky like a trembling white finger, searching for him, and archie began to illuminate the surrounding blackness.

Mark, the ever-practical, was calmly preparing for the inevitable end, and even in that desperate moment Biggles wondered if there was anything that could shake Mark out of his habitual calmness. He picked up the machine-guns, one after the other, and threw them overboard; the Huns would be welcome to what was left of them after their eight-hundred-foot fall. The ammunition drums followed. He tore up his maps, threw them into the air and watched them swirl away aft.

Biggles felt in the canvas pocket inside the cockpit, then took out his own maps, ripped them across, and sent the pieces after Mark's. He thrust his loaded Very pistol into his pocket in readiness to send a shot into the petrol tank of the machine as soon as they were on the ground—providing they were not knocked out in the crash.

The destruction of his machine to prevent it falling into the hands of the enemy is the first duty of an airman who lands in hostile territory.

The sky around them became an inferno of darting flames and hurtling metal. Several pieces of shrapnel struck the machine, and it quivered like a terrified horse. Once the F.E. was nearly turned upside down by a terrific explosion under the port wingtip. 400—300—200 feet ran the altimeter. Mark was leaning over the side staring into the blackness below them.

Biggles could distinguish nothing; the earth looked like a dark indigo stain, broken only by the flashes of the guns and the intermittent spurts of machine-guns. He no longer looked at his altimeter, for he knew he was too low for it to be of any assistance; he could only keep his eyes glued below and hope for the best.

Suddenly, the shadow that was the earth swept up to meet him. He pulled the joy-stick back until the machine was flying on even keel. It began to sink as it lost flying speed, then staggered like a wounded animal. He lifted his knees to his chin, covered his face with his arms, and waited for the end. For a moment there was silence, broken only by the faint hum of the wires and the rumble of the guns.

Crash! With a crunching, tearing, rending scream of protest, the machine struck the ground, and subsided in a heap of debris. The nacelle, in which the crew sat, buried its nose into the earth, reared up, then turned turtle.

Biggles soared through space and landed with a dull squelch in a sea of mud, but he had scrambled to his feet in an instant, wiping the slime from his eyes with the backs of his gauntlets.

"Mark—Mark!" he hissed. "Where are you, Mark? Are you hurt, old man?"

"Hold hard, I'm coming! Don't make such a row, you fool!" snarled Mark, dragging himself clear of the debris and unwinding a wire that had coiled around his neck.

Rat-tat-tat-tat. Rat-tat-tat-tat.

A Very light soared upwards, and half a dozen machine-guns began their vicious stutter somewhere near at hand; bullets began splintering into the tangled wreck of the machine and zipping into the mud like a swarm of angry hornets.

"Come on, let's get out of this!" gasped Mark. "Run for it; the artillery will open up any second!"

"Run! Where to?" panted Biggles.

"Anywhere—to get away from here!" snapped Mark, slithering and sliding through the ooze.

Wee-e-e—Bang! The first shell arrived with the noise of an express train and exploded with a roar like the end of the world. Biggles took a flying leap into a shell-hole and wormed his way into the mud at the bottom like a mole. He grunted as Mark landed on top of him.

"Why—the dickens—don't you look—where you're going!" he spluttered, as they squelched side by side in the sludge; while the shell-torn earth rocked under the onslaught from the artillery.

"We're all right here," announced Mark firmly. "They say a shell never lands in the same place twice."

"I wish I knew that for a fact," muttered Biggles. "This is what comes of night-flying. Night birds, eh? Great jumping mackerel, we're a couple of owls all right; an owl's got enough sense to stay——"

"Shut up!" snarled Mark, as the bombardment grew less intense, and then suddenly died away. "Let's see where we are," he whispered, as an eerie silence settled over the scene.

"See where we are? Have you any idea where we are?"

"Hark!"

They held their breaths and listened, but no sound reached their ears.

"I thought I heard someone coming," breathed Mark. "This is

A line of bayonets and then a body of men rose up in the darkness at the edge of the trench

awful, not knowing which side of the Lines we're on!"

They crept up to the lip of the shell-crater and stared into the surrounding darkness. A Very light soared upwards from a spot about a hundred yards away. Biggles, peering under his hand in the glare, distinctly saw a belt of barbed wire a few yards away on their left. Mark, who was looking in the other direction, gripped his arm in a vice-like clutch.

"Huns!" he whispered. "There's a party of them coming this way. I could tell them by the shape of their helmets. Come on, this way!"

They started crawling warily towards the wire, but when they reached it, finding no opening, they commenced crawling parallel with it, freezing into a death-like stillness whenever a Very light cast its weird glow over the scene.

"Those Huns were coming from the opposite direction, so this should be our side," muttered Mark.

"Don't talk," whispered Biggles, "let's keep going—this looks like a gap in the wire."

By lying flat on the ground so that the obstruction was silhouetted against the sky, they could see a break in the ten feet wide belt of barbed wire, where it had evidently been torn up by shell-fire. They crawled through the breach, then paused to listen with straining ears.

"I can hear someone talking ahead of us; they must be in a trench," whispered Mark.

"So can I; let's get closer," whispered Biggles. "Ssh—there it is! I can see the parapet. We shall have to go carefully, or we may be shot by our own fellows." He raised himself on his hands and was about to call out—in fact, he had opened his mouth to do so—when a sound reached their ears that seemed to freeze the blood in their veins.

It was a harsh, coarse voice, speaking in a language they did not understand, but which they had no difficulty in recognizing as German. It came from the parapet a few yards in front of them.

A line of bayonets and then a body of men rose up in the darkness at the edge of the trench; there was no mistaking the coal-scuttle helmets.

Neither of the airmen spoke; as one man they sank to the ground, forcing themselves into the cold mud, and lay motionless. Heavy footsteps squelched through the mud towards them; a voice was speaking in a low undertone. Nearer and nearer they came, until Biggles felt the muscles of his back retract to receive the stabbing pain of a bayonet-thrust. He nearly cried out as a heavy foot descended on his hand, but his gauntlet and the soft mud under it saved the bones from being broken. The German stumbled, recovered, half-glanced over his shoulder to see what had tripped him; but, seeing what he supposed to be a corpse, turned and walked quickly after the others.

"Phew!" gasped Biggles, as the footsteps receded into the distance.

"Let's get out of this!" muttered Mark. "They may be back any moment. Another minute and we should have walked straight into their trench. Hark!"

The musical hum of an F.E. reached their ears, and although they could not see it they could follow its path of flight by the archie bursts and the sound. It was coming from the direction of the German trench. It passed straight over them, the archie died away, and presently the sound faded into the night.

"That's one of our fellows going home, so it gives us our direction if we can only find a way through our own wire. If there isn't a gap, we're sunk; so we might crawl along this blinking wire to Switzerland!"

"Ssh!"

Once more the sound of footsteps reached them from somewhere near at hand, but they could see nothing.

"I can't stand much more of this!" growled Biggles. "It's giving me the creeps. I've just crawled over somebody—or something that was somebody."

Bang! They both jumped and then lay flat as another Very light curved high into the air; in its dazzling light Biggles distinctly saw a group of German soldiers, evidently a patrol, standing quite still, not more than fifty yards away. Suddenly he remembered something. He groped in his pocket, whipped out his own Very pistol, took careful aim, and fired. The light in the air went out at the same moment. The shot from Biggles' pistol dropped in the mud a hundred yards away, where it lay hissing in a cloud of red smoke that changed gradually to a ghastly, livid green.

"You fool, what are you at?" snarled Mark. "I thought I was shot."

"Didn't you see those Huns? I bet I've made them jump!"

"They'll probably make us jump in a minute!" retorted Mark.

"Would have done if I hadn't fired that Very light at 'em, you mean!" retorted Biggles. "Nothing like getting in the first shot. Makes the other fellow scary. We've been walked over by one crowd and treated as bloomin' doormats. I don't want a second dose of that!"

"You'll get a dose of something else if those Huns poodle along here to inquire what the fireworks are for!" replied Mark.

"If!" jeered Biggles. "I'll bet those chaps are legging it for home for all they're worth. An' I don't blame 'em. I'd do the same myself if I jolly well knew where home was."

"You'll never live to see home again if you don't stop playing the silly ass!" growled Mark. "And now shut up and listen. See if you can hear anybody talking in a language we understand."

For some time the two airmen remained still, lying on the ground and listening intently for the sound of voices. But they could hear nothing save the occasional banging of rifles. At last Biggles grew impatient.

"Well, I'm not going to stay messing about here any longer!" he snapped. "We'll settle things one way or the other. It will start to get light presently, and then we're done for. I believe that's our wire just in front of us. What about letting out a shout to see if our fellows are within earshot?"

"The Huns will hear us, too."

"I can't help that. Hold tight, I'm going to yell. Hallo, there!" he bellowed. "Is anybody about?"

A reply came from a spot so close that Biggles instinctively ducked.

"What are you bleating abart?" said a Cockney voice calmly. "You come any closer to me and I'll give you somethink to holler for. You can't catch me on that hop!"

Bang! A rifle blazed in the darkness, not ten yards away, and a bullet whistled past Biggles' head.

"Hi! That's enough of that!" he shouted. "We're British officers, I tell you—fliers. We crashed outside the wire and can't get through. Come and show us the way!"

"Why didn't you say so before?" came the reply. "You might 'ave got 'urt. 'Old 'ard a minute! But you keep your 'ands up, and no half-larks!"

Silence fell.

"He's either coming himself, or he's gone to fetch someone," muttered Mark. "We can't blame him for being suspicious. He must have been in a listening-post, which is where people shoot first and ask questions afterwards. The Huns get up to all sorts of tricks."

"Where are you, you fellows?" suddenly said a quiet voice near them.

"Here we are!" answered Biggles.

"Stand fast—I'm coming."

An officer, revolver in hand, closely followed by half a dozen Tommies wearing the unmistakable British tin helmets, loomed up suddenly in the darkness.

"How many of you are there?" said the voice.

"Two," replied Biggles shortly.

"All right, follow me—and don't make a row about it."

Squelching through the ooze, they followed the officer through a zigzag track in the wire. The Tommies closed in behind them. A trench, from which projected a line of bayonets, lay across their path, but at a word from their escort the rifles were lowered, and the two airmen half slipped and half scrambled into the trench. The beam of a flash-lamp cut through the darkness and went slowly over their faces and uniforms.

"You look a couple of pretty scarecrows, I must say," said a voice, with a chuckle. "Come into my dugout and have a rest. I'll send a runner to headquarters with a request that they ring up your squadron and tell them you're safe. What have you been up to?"

"Oh—er—night-flying, that's all. Just night-flying!" said Biggles airily.

The Pup's First Fight

When the time came for Biggles to leave his old squadron and say good-bye to Mark Way, his gunner, he found himself a good deal more depressed than he had thought possible; he realized for the first time just how attached to them he had become. Naturally, though, he had been delighted to join a scout squadron, for he had always wanted to fly single-seaters. The presence of his old pal, Mahoney, who was Flight-Commander, prevented any awkwardness or strangeness amongst his new comrades, and he quickly settled down to routine work.

The commanding officer, Major Mullen, of his new squadron, No. 266, stationed at Maranique, allowed none of his pilots to take unnecessary risks if he could prevent it. So he gave Biggles ten days in which to make himself proficient in the handling of the single-seater Pup that had been allocated to him.

Biggles was told to put in as much flying-time as possible, but on no account to cross the Lines, and he found that the enforced rest from eternal vigilance did him a power of good, for his nerves had been badly jarred by his late spell of trench strafing.

By the end of a week he was thoroughly at home with the Pup, and ready to try his hand at something more serious than beetling up and down behind his own Lines. He had noted all the outstanding landmarks around Maranique, and once or twice he accompanied Mahoney on practice formation flights. His Flight-Commander had expressed himself satisfied, and Biggles begged to do a "show".

His chance came soon. Lorton was wounded in the arm and packed off to hospital, and Biggles was detailed to take his place the following morning. But the afternoon before this decision took effect he had what he regarded as a slice of luck that greatly enhanced his reputation with the C.O., and the officers of the squadron, as well as bringing his name before Wing Headquarters.

He had set off on a cross-country flight to the Aircraft Repair Section at St. Omer, to make inquiries for the equipment officer about a machine that had gone back for reconditioning, when he spotted a line of white archie bursts at a very high altitude—about 15,000 feet, he judged it to be.

He was flying at about 5,000 a few miles inside the Lines at the time, and he knew that the archie was being fired by British guns, which could only mean that the target was an enemy aircraft. It seemed to be flying on a course parallel with the Lines, evidently on a photographic or scouting raid.

Without any real hope of overtaking it he set off in pursuit, and, knowing that sooner or later the German would have to turn to reach his own side he steered an oblique course that would bring him between the raider and the Lines. In a few minutes he had increased his height to 10,000 feet, and could distinctly see the enemy machine. It was a Rumpler two-seater. He had no doubt that the observer had spotted him, but the machine continued on its way as if the pilot was not concerned, possibly by reason of his superior altitude.

Biggles began to edge a little nearer to the Lines, and was not much more than a thousand feet below the Hun, when, to his disgust, it turned slowly and headed off on a diagonal course towards No Man's Land.

The Pup was climbing very slowly now, and it was more with hope than confidence that Biggles continued the pursuit. Then the unexpected happened. The enemy pilot turned sharply and dived straight at him, but opened fire at much too great a range for it to be effective, although he held the burst for at least a hundred rounds. Biggles had no idea where the bullets went, but he saw the Hun, at the end of his dive, zoom nearly back to his original altitude, and then make for home at full speed. But he had lingered just a trifle too long.

Biggles climbed up into the "blind" spot under the enemy's elevators, and although the range was still too long for good shooting, he opened fire. Whether any of his shots took effect he was unable to tell, but the Hun was evidently alarmed, for the Rumpler made a quick turn out of the line of fire. It was a clumsy turn, and cost him two hundred precious feet of height at a moment when height was all-important. Moreover, it did not give the gunner in the back seat a chance to use his weapon.

Biggles seized his opportunity, and fired one of the longest bursts he ever fired in his life. The German gunner swayed for a moment, then collapsed in his cockpit. Then, to his intense satisfaction, Biggles saw the propeller of the other machine slow down and stop, whereupon the enemy pilot shoved his nose down and dived for the Lines, now not more than two or three miles away.

It was a move that suited Biggles well, for the Rumpler was defenceless from the rear, so he tore down in hot pursuit, guns blazing, knowing that the Hun was at his mercy. The enemy pilot seemed to realize this for he turned broadside on and threw up his hands in surrender.

Biggles was amazed, for although he had heard of such things being done, it was his first experience of it. He ceased firing at once and took up a position on the far side of the disabled machine; he did not trust his prisoner very much, for he guessed that he would, if the opportunity arose, make a dash for the Lines—so near, and yet so far away. Biggles therefore shepherded him down like a well-trained sheep-dog bringing in a stray lamb.

He could not really find it in his heart to blame the enemy pilot for surrendering. The fellow had had to choose between being made a prisoner and certain death, and had chosen captivity as the lesser of the two evils. "Death before capture," is no doubt an admirable slogan, but it loses some of its attractiveness in the face of cold facts.

The German landed about four miles from Maranique and was

prevented by a crowd of Tommies from purposely injuring his machine. Biggles landed in a nearby field and hurried to the scene, arriving just as the C.O. and several officers of the squadron, who had witnessed the end of the combat from the aerodrome, dashed up in the squadron car. It was purely a matter of luck that Major Raymond, of Wing Headquarters, who had been on the aerodrome talking with Major Mullen, was with them.

He smiled at Biggles approvingly. "Good show!" he said. "We've been trying to get hold of one of these machines intact for a long time."

Biggles made a suitable reply and requested that the crew of the Rumpler should be well cared for. The pilot, whose name they learnt was Schmidt, looked morose and bad-tempered—as, indeed, he had every cause to be; the observer had been wounded in the chest and was unconscious.

They were taken away under escort in an ambulance, and that was the end of the affair. Biggles never learnt what happened to them.

The offensive patrol for which he had been detailed in place of Lorton turned out to be a more difficult business. It began quite simply. He took his place in a formation of five machines, and for an hour or more they cruised up and down their sector without incident, except, of course, for the inevitable archie. Then the trouble started around a single machine.

Several times they had passed a British machine—an R.E.8—circling over the same spot, obviously engaged in doing a shoot for the artillery, and Biggles was able to sympathize with the pilot. He watched the circling plane quite dispassionately for a moment or two, glanced away, and then turned back to the R.E.8. It was no longer there.

He stared—and stared harder. Then he saw it, three thousand feet below, plunging earthwards in flames. Screwing his head round a little farther, he made out three German Albatross planes streaking for home. They must have made their attack on the two-seater under the very noses of the Pups, and, well satisfied with the result of their work, were removing themselves from the vicinity without loss of time. But they were well below the Pups, and Mahoney, who was leading, tore down after them in a screaming dive, closely followed by the rest of the formation.

As they went down, something—he could not say what—made Biggles, who was an outside flank man, look back over his shoulder. There was really no reason why he should but the fact that he did so provided another example of the uncanny instinct he was developing for detecting the presence of Huns.

The sight that met his gaze put all thought of the escaping Albatrosses clean out of his head. A German High Patrol of not fewer than twenty triplanes was coming down like the proverbial ton of bricks.

Biggles' first idea was to warn Mahoney of the impending onslaught, but, try as he would, he could not overtake his leader. Yet he knew that if the Huns were allowed to come on in a solid formation on their tails, most of them would be wiped out before they knew what had hit them. He could think of only one thing to do, and he did it, although it did not occur to him that he was making something very much like a deliberate sacrifice of his own life. That he was not killed was due no doubt to the very unexpectedness of his move, which temporarily disorganized the Hun "circus". He swung the Pup round on its axis, cocked up his nose to face the oncoming Huns, and let drive at the whole formation.

The leader swerved just in time to avoid head-on collision. His wing tip missed Biggles' by inches. The lightning turn threw the others out of their places, and they, too, had to swerve wildly to avoid collision with their leader.

Biggles held his breath as the cloud of gaudy-coloured enemy machines roared past him, so close that he could see the faces of the pilots staring at him. Yet not a bullet touched his machine. Nor did he hit one of them—at least, as far as he could see.

The Huns pulled up, hesitating, to see if their leader was going on after the other Pups or staying to slay the impudent one. At that

The leader swerved just in time to avoid head-on collision

moment, Mahoney, missing one of his men, looked back. In that quick flash it must have seemed to him that Biggles was taking on the entire German Air Force single-handed, and he hung his Pup on its prop as he headed back towards the mêlée.

He knew what Biggles himself at that time did not know; that the German formation was the formidable Richthofen "circus", led by the famous Baron himself, his conspicuous all-red plane even then pouring lead at the lone Pup.

Biggles could never afterwards describe the sensation of finding himself in the middle of Germany's most noted air fighters. He was, as he put it, completely flummoxed. He merely shot at every machine that swam across his sights, wondering all the while why his Pup did not fall to pieces.

The reason why it did not was probably that put forward by Captain Albert Ball, V.C., in defence of his method of plunging headlong into the middle of an enemy circus. Such tactics temporarily disorganized the enemy formation, and the pilots dared not shoot as freely as they would normally for fear of hitting or colliding with their own men. Be that as it may, in the opening stage of the uproar Biggles' Pup was hit less than a dozen times, and in no place was it seriously damaged.

By the time the Huns sorted themselves out Mahoney and the other three Pups were on the scene. Even so, the gallant action of the leader in taking on such overwhelming odds would not have availed had it not been for the opportune arrival of a second formation of Pups and a squadron of Bristols—Biggles' old squadron, although he did not know it. That turned the tide.

The huge dog-fight lost height quickly, as such affairs nearly always did, and was soon down to five thousand feet. It was impossible for any pilot to know exactly what was happening; each man picked an opponent and stuck to him as long as he could. If he lost him he turned to find another.

That was precisely what Biggles did, and it was utterly out of the question for him to see if he shot anyone down. If a machine at which he was shooting fell out of the fight, someone else was shooting at him before he could determine whether his Hun was really hit or merely shamming.

He saw more than one machine spinning, and two or three smoke-trails where others had gone down in flames. He also saw a Bristol and a triplane that had collided whirling down together in a last ghastly embrace.

At four thousand feet he pulled out, slightly dizzy, and tried to make out what was happening. He picked out Mahoney by his streamers, not far away, and noted that the fight seemed to be breaking up by mutual consent. Odd machines were still circling round each other, but each leader was trying to rally his men.

Mahoney, in particular, was trying frantically to attract the attention of the surviving members of his patrol, for the fight had drifted over German territory, and it was high time to see about getting nearer the Lines.

Biggles took up position on Mahoney's flank, and presently another Pup joined them. Of the other two there was no sign.

The Bristols were already streaming back towards home in open formation, and Mahoney followed them. They passed the charred remains of the R.E.8 that had been the cause of all the trouble, gaunt and black in the middle of No Man's Land. They reached the Lines and turned to fly parallel with them.

Their patrol was not yet finished, but all the machines had been more or less damaged, so after waiting a few minutes to give the other two Pups a chance of joining them if they were still in the air, they turned towards the aerodrome. It was as well they did, for Biggles' engine began to give trouble, although by nursing it he managed to reach home.

They discovered that the squadron had already been informed of the dog-fight, artillery observers along the Line reporting that five British and seven German machines had been seen to fall. There seemed little chance of the two missing Pups turning up. The surviving members of the patrol hung about the tarmac for some time, but they did not return. That evening they were reported "missing".

266 Squadron was re-equipped with Sopwith Camels in the Spring of 1917.—Ed.

The Zone Call

Oh, my batman awoke me from my bed;
I'd had a thick night and I'd got a sore head;
  So I said to myself,
  To myself I said,
Oh, I haven't got a hope in the mo--orning.

So I went to the sheds to examine my gun,
And then my engine I tried to run,
  But the revs she ga-ve
  Were a thousand to one,
So I hadn't got a hope in the mo--orning.

The words of the old R.F.C. song, roared by forty youthful voices to the tune of "John Peel", drowned the accompaniment of the cracked mess piano in spite of the strenuous efforts of the pianist.

Biggles pushed the hair off his forehead. "Lord, it's hot in here; I'm going outside," he said to Wilkinson of 287 Squadron.

The two officers rose and strolled slowly towards the door. It was still daylight, but a thick layer of thundercloud hung low in the sky, making the atmosphere oppressive.

Oh, we were escorting "twenty-two,"
Hadn't got a notion what to do,
  So we shot down a Spa-a-d,
  And an S.E. too,
For we hadn't—

"Stop!" Biggles had bounded back into the centre of the room and held up his arms for silence. "Hark!"

At the expression on his face a sudden hush fell upon the assembly, and the next instant forty officers had stiffened into attitudes of tense expectancy as a low vibrating hum filled the air. It was the unmistakable "pour-vous, pour-vous" of a Mercédès aero-engine, low down, not far away.

"A Hun!" The silence was broken by a wild yell and the crash of falling chairs as Biggles darted through the open door and streaked like a madman for the sheds, shouting orders as he went. The ack-emmas had needed no warning; a Camel was already on the tarmac; others were being wheeled out with feverish speed. Capless and goggleless, tunic still thrown open at the throat, Biggles made a flying leap into the cockpit of the first Camel, and within a minute, in spite of Wilkinson's plaintive "Wait for me", was tearing down-wind across the sunbaked aerodrome in a cloud of dust.

He was in the air, climbing back up over the sheds, before the second machine was ready to take off. The clouds were low, and at 1,000 feet the grey mist was swirling in his slipstream. He could no longer hear the enemy plane, for the roar of his Bentley Rotary drowned all other sound. He pushed his joystick forward for a moment to gather speed and then pulled it back in a swift zoom. Bursting out into the sunlight above he literally flung the machine round in a lightning righthand turn to avoid crashing into a Pfalz scout, painted vivid scarlet with white stripes behind the pilot's seat.

"My God!" muttered Biggles, startled. "I nearly rammed him."

He was round in a second, warming his guns as he came. The Pfalz had turned, too, and was now circling erratically in a desperate effort to avoid the glittering pencil lines of tracer that started at the muzzles of Biggles' guns and ended at the tail of the Boche machine. The German pilot made no attempt to retaliate, but concentrated on dodging the hail of lead, waving his left arm above his head. Biggles ceased firing and looked about him suspiciously, but not another enemy machine was in sight.

"Come on; let's get it over," he muttered, as he thumbed his triggers again; but the Boche put his nose down and dived through the cloud, Biggles close behind him.

They emerged below the cloud bank in the same relative positions, and it at once became obvious that the German intended to land on the aerodrome, but a brisk burst of machine-gun fire from the Lewis guns in front of the mess caused him to change his mind; instead, he hopped over the hedge and made a clumsy landing in the next field. Biggles landed close behind him and ran towards the pilot, now struggling to get a box of matches from his inside pocket to fire the machine.

Biggles seized him by the collar and threw him clear.

"Speak English?" he snapped.

"Yes."

"What's the matter with you? Haven't you got any guns?" sneered the British pilot, noting the German's pale face.

"Nein, no guns," said the German quickly.

"What?"

The German shrugged his shoulders and pointed. A swift glance showed Biggles that such was indeed his case.

"My God!" he cried, aghast. "You people running short of weapons or something? We'd better lend you some."

"I vas lost," said the German pilot, resignedly. "I am to take a new Pfalz to Lille, but the clouds—I cannot see. The benzine is nearly finish. You come—I come down, so."

"Tough luck," admitted Biggles as a crowd of officers and ack-emmas arrived on the scene at the double. "Well, come and have a drink—you've butted into a party."

"Huh! No wonder your crowd scores if you go about shooting at delivery pilots," grinned Wilkinson, who had just landed.

"You go and stick your face in an oil sump, Wilks," cried Biggles hotly. "How did I know he hadn't any guns?"

. . .

Biggles sprang lightly from the squadron tender and looked at

Biggles landed close behind him and ran towards the pilot

the deserted aerodrome in astonishment. It was the morning following his encounter with the unarmed Pfalz. For some days a tooth had been troubling him, and on the advice of the Medical Officer he had been to Clarmes to have the offending molar extracted. He had not hurried back, as the M.O. had forbidden him to fly that day, and now he had returned to find every machine except his own in the air.

"Where have they all gone, Flight?" he asked the Flight-Sergeant.

"Dunno, sir. The C.O. came out in a hurry about an hour ago and they all went off together," replied the N.C.O.

"Just my luck," grumbled Biggles, "trust something to happen when I'm away for a few hours! Oh, well!"

He made his way to the squadron office, where he found Tyler, commonly known as "Wat", the Recording Officer, busy with some papers.

"What's on, Wat?" asked Biggles.

"Escort."

"Escorting what?"

"You remember that Hun you got yesterday?"

Biggles nodded.

"Well, apparently he was three sheets in the wind when Wing came and fetched him. He blabbed a whole lot of news to the Intelligence people. This is what he told 'em. He said that three new Staffels were being formed at Lagnicourt. A whole lot of new machines were being sent there; in fact, when he was there two days ago, over thirty machines were being assembled."

"Funny, him letting a thing like that drop," interrupted Biggles. "He didn't strike me as being blotto, either. He drank practically nothing."

"Well, Wing says he was tight as a lord, and bragged that the three new circuses were going to wipe us off the map, so they decided to nip the plot in the bud. They've sent every machine they can get into the air with a full load of bombs to fan the whole caboodle sky-high—all the Fours, Nines, and Biffs[1] have gone, and even the R.E.8s they can spare from Art. Obs.[2] Two-eight-seven, two-nine-nine and our people are escorting 'em."

"Well, they can have it," said Biggles cheerfully. "Escorting's a mouldy business, anyway. Thanks, Wat."

He strolled out onto the aerodrome, gently rubbing his lacerated jaw, and catching sight of the German machine now standing on the tarmac made his way slowly towards it. He examined it with interest, for a complete ready-to-fly-away Boche machine was a *rara avis*. He slipped his hand into the map case, but the maps had been removed. His finger felt and closed around a torn piece of paper at the bottom of the lining; it was creased as if it had been roughly torn off and used to mark a fold in a map. Biggles glanced at it disinterestedly, noting some typewritten matter on it, but as it was in German and conveyed nothing to him he was about to throw it away when the Flight-Sergeant passed near him.

"Do you speak German, Flight?" called Biggles.

"No, sir, but Thompson does; he used to be in the Customs Office or something like that," replied the N.C.O.

"Ask him to come here a minute, will you?" said Biggles.

"Can you tell me what that says?" he asked a moment later, as an ack-emma approached him and saluted.

The airman took the paper and looked at it for a minute without speaking. "It's an extract from some orders, sir," he said at length. "The first part of it's gone, but this is what it says, roughly speaking: 'With effect'—there's a bit gone there—'any flieger'—flyer, that is—'falling into the hands of the enemy will therefore repeat that three Jagdstaffels are being assembled at Lagni——' Can't read the place, sir. 'By doing so, he will be doing service by assisting'—can't read that, sir. It ends, 'Expires on July 21st at twelve, midnight. This order must on no account be taken into the air.' That's all, sir."

"Read that again," said Biggles slowly.

After the airman had obeyed, Biggles returned to the Squadron Office deep in thought. He put a call through to Wing Headquarters

[1]Bristol Fighters. [2]Artillery Observation.

and asked for Colonel Raymond.

"That you, sir? Bigglesworth here," he said, as the Colonel's crisp voice answered him. "About this big raid, sir. Do you mind if I ask whether you know for certain that these Boche machines are at Lagnicourt?"

"Yes; we made reconnaissance at dawn, and the observer reported several machines in various stages of erection on the tarmac. Why do you ask?"

"I've just found a bit of paper in the Pfalz that Boche brought over. I can't read it because it's in German, but I've had it translated, and it looks as if that Hun had orders to tell you that tale. Will you send over for it?"

"I'll send a messenger for it right away, but I shouldn't worry about it; the Huns are there; we've seen them. Goodbye."

Biggles hung the receiver up slowly and turned to Wat, who had listened to the conversation.

"You'll get shot one day ringing up the Wing like that!" he said reprovingly.

"It would be a hell of a joke to send forty machines to drop twenty thousand quids' worth of bombs on a lot of obsolete spare parts," mused Biggles, "but there's more in it than that. The Boche wants our machines out of the way. Why? That's what I want to know. Lagnicourt lies thirty miles north-west of here. I fancy it wouldn't be a bad idea if somebody went and had a dekko what the Huns were doing in the north-east. Even my gross intelligence tells me that when a Hun is told what he's got to say when he's shot down, there's something fishy about it."

"The M.O. says you're not to fly today," protested the R.O.

"Rot! What the hell does he think I fly with, my teeth?" asked Biggles sarcastically. "See you later."

Within ten minutes Biggles was in the air, heading into the blue roughly north-east of the aerodrome. An unusual amount of archie marked his progress and he noticed it with satisfaction, for it tended to confirm his suspicions.

"What ho!" he addressed the invisible gunner. "So you don't want any Peeping Toms about today, eh? Want to discourage me."

The archie became really hot, and twice he had to circle to spoil the gunner's aim. He kept a watchful eye on the ground below, but saw nothing unusual.

He passed over an R.E.8 spotting for the artillery, manfully plodding its monotonous figure-of-eight 3,000 feet below, and nodded sympathetically. Presently he altered his course a little westerly and the archie faded away. "Don't mind me going that way, eh? Well, let's try the other way again," he muttered. Instantly the air was thick with black, oily bursts of smoke, and Biggles nodded understandingly. "So I'm getting warm, am I?" he mused. "They might as well say so; what imaginations they've got."

Straight ahead of him, lying like a great dark green stain across the landscape, lay the forest of Duvigny. Keeping a watchful eye above for enemy aircraft, he looked at it closely, but there was no sign of anything unusual about its appearance.

"I wonder if that's it," he mused, deep in thought. "I could soon find out; it's risky, but it's the only way."

He knew what all old pilots knew, a trick the German pilots had learned early in the war, when vast numbers of Russian troops were concealed in the forests along the north-German frontier, and that was, that if an enemy plane flew low enough, the troops, no matter how well hidden, would reveal their presence by shooting at it. Not even strict orders could prevent troops from firing at an enemy aeroplane within range.

He pushed his stick foward and went roaring down at the forest. At 1,000 feet he started pulling out, but not before he had seen several hundred twinkling fire-flies amongst the greenery. The fireflies were, of course, the flashes of rifles aimed at him. In one place a number of men had run out into a little clearing and started firing, but an officer had driven them back.

"So that's it, is it?" muttered Biggles, thrilling with excitement. "I wonder how many of them there are."

Time and time again he dived low over different parts of the

He flew close beside the R.E.8, raised his arm above his head, and, with some difficulty, sent a series of dots and dashes

forest and each time the twinkling flashes betrayed the hidden troops. His wings were holed in many places, but he heeded them not. It would take a lucky shot from a rifle to bring him down.

"My God!" he muttered, as he pulled up at the far end of the forest, after his tenth dive, "the wood's full of 'em. There must be fifty thousand men lying in that timber, and it's close to the Line. They're massing for a big attack. What did those orders say? July 21st? Great God, that's tomorrow. They'll attack this afternoon, or at latest tonight. I'd better be getting out of this. So that's why they didn't want any of our machines prowling about."

He made for the Line, toying with the fine adjustment to get the very last rev. out of his engine. He could see the R.E.8 still tapping out its "G.G." (fire) signal to the gunners and marking the position of the falling shells, and the sight of it gave him an idea. The R.E.8 was fitted with wireless; he was not. If only he could get the pilot to send out a zone call[1] on that wood, his work was done.

Biggles flew close to the R.E.8, signalling to attract attention. How could he tell them, that was the problem. He flew closer and gesticulated wildly, jabbing downwards towards the wood, and then tapping with his finger on an invisible key. The pilot and observer eyed him stupidly and Biggles shrugged his shoulders in despair. Then inspiration struck him. He knew the Morse Code, of course, for every pilot had to pass a test in it before going to France. He flew close beside the R.E.8, raised his arm above his head, and, with some difficulty, sent a series of dots and dashes. He saw the observer nod understandingly and grab a notebook to take down the message. Biggles started his signal. Dash, dash, dot, dot—Z, dash, dash, dash—O, dash, dot—N, dot—E. He continued the performance until he had sent the words, "Zone Call, Wood," and then stabbed viciously at the wood with his forefinger. He saw the observer lean forward and have a quick, difficult conversation with the pilot, who

[1] A Zone Call was a special call from an aircraft to the artillery and was only used in very exceptional circumstances. When the zone call was tapped out by the wireless operator it was followed by the pin-point of the target. Every weapon of every calibre in range directed rapid fire on the spot.—Ed.

nodded. The observer raised both thumbs in the air and bent over his buzzer. Biggles turned away to watch the result.

Within a minute he saw the first shell explode in the centre of the wood. Another followed it, then another and another. In five minutes the place was an inferno of fire, smoke, flying timber and hurtling steel, and thousands of figures, clad in the field-grey of the German infantry, were swarming out into the open to escape the pulverizing bombardment. He could see the officers attempting to get the men into some sort of order, but there was no stemming that wild panic. They poured into the communication trenches, and others, unable to find cover, were flinging away their equipment and running for their lives.

"Holy mackerel, what a sight!" murmured Biggles. "What a pity the Colonel isn't here to see it."

A Bristol Fighter appeared in the sky above him, heading for the scene of carnage. The observer was leaning over the side and the pilot's arm was steadily moving up and down as he exposed plate after plate in his camera.

"He'll have to believe me when he sees those photographs, though," thought Biggles. "Well, I should think I've saved our chaps in the Line a lot of trouble," he soliloquised, as he turned to congratulate the R.E.8 crew, but the machine was far away. Biggles' Camel suddenly rocked violently and he realized the reason for the R.E.8's swift departure. He was right in the line of fire of the artillery and the shells were passing near him. He put his nose down in a fright and sped towards home in the wake of the R.E.8.

He landed on the aerodrome to find the escorting Camels had returned, and the pilots greeted him noisily.

"Had a nice trip, chaps?" inquired Biggles.

"No," growled Mahoney; "didn't see a Hun the whole way out and home. These escorts bore me stiff. What have you been doing?"

"Oh, having a little fun and games on my own."

"Who with?"

"With the German Army," said Biggles lightly.

In five minutes the place was an inferno of fire, smoke, flying timber and hurtling steel

Biggles was promoted to Captain and made a flight-commander soon after he joined 266 Squadron.—Ed.

The Boob

Mahoney, on his way to the sheds to take his Flight off for an Ordinary Patrol, paused in his stride as his eye fell on Biggles leaning in an attitude of utter boredom against the doorstep of the officers' mess.

"Why so pensive, young aviator?" he smiled. "Has Mr Cox grabbed your pay to square up the overdraft?" he added, as he caught sight of an open letter in the other's hand.

"Worse than that; much, much worse," replied Biggles. "Couldn't be worse in fact—what do you think of this?"

He held out the letter.

"I haven't the time to read it, laddie. What's the trouble?"

"Oh, it's from an elderly female relative of mine. She says her son—my cousin—is in the R.F.C. on his way to France. She's pulled the wires at the Air Board for the Pool to send him to 266, as she feels sure I can take care of him. She asks me to see that he changes his laundry regularly, doesn't drink, doesn't get mixed up with the French minxes, and a dozen other 'doesn'ts!' My God! it's a bit thick; what the hell does she think this is—a prep. school?"

"What's he like?"

"I don't know; it's years since I saw him; and if he's anything like the little horror he was then, God help us—and him. His Christian names are Algernon Montgomery, and that's just what he looked like—a slice of warmed-up death wrapped in velvet and ribbons."

"Sounds pretty ghastly. When's he coming?"

"Today, apparently. His name's on the notice-board. The old girl had the brass face to write to the C.O., and he's posted him to my Flight—in revenge, I expect."

"Too bad," replied Mahoney, sympathetically. "Well, go and get the letter done, telling her how bravely he died, and forget about it. There comes the tender now—see you later."

Biggles, left alone, watched the tender pull up and discharge two new pilots and their kit; he had no difficulty in recognizing his new charge, who approached eagerly.

"You're Biggles—aren't you? I know you from the photo at home."

The matured edition of the youth was even more unprepossessing than Biggles expected. His uniform was dirty, his hair long, his face, which wore a permanent expression of amused surprise, was a mass of freckles.

"My name's Captain Bigglesworth," said the Flight-Commander coldly. "You are posted to my Flight. Get your kit into your room, report to the squadron office, and then come back here; I want to have a word with you."

"Sorry, sir," said Algernon apologetically; "of course, I forgot."

A few minutes later he rejoined Biggles in the mess.

"What'll you have to drink?" invited Biggles.

"Have you any ginger ale?"

"I shouldn't think so," replied Biggles. "We don't get much demand for it. Have you any ginger ale, Adams?" he asked the mess waiter—"I'll have the usual."

"Yes, sir, I think I've got one somewhere, if I can find it," replied the waiter, looking at the newcomer curiously.

"Sit down and let's talk," said Biggles, when the drinks had been served. "How much flying have you done?"

"Fourteen hours on Avro's and ten on Camels."

"Ten hours, eh?" mused Biggles. "Ten hours. So they're sending 'em out here with ten hours now. My God! Now listen," he went on; "I want you to forget those ten hours. This is where you'll learn to

"That's all. Can you remember that?"

fly—they can't teach you at home. If you live a week you'll begin to know something about it. I don't want to discourage you, but most people who come out here live on an average twenty-four hours. If you survive a week you're fairly safe. I can't teach you much; nobody can; you'll find things out for yourself.

"First of all, never cross the Line alone under 10,000 feet—not yet, anyway. Never go more than a couple of miles over unless you are with a formation. Never go down after a Hun. If you see a Hun looking like easy meat, make for home like Hell, and if that Hun fires a Very light, kick out your foot and slam the stick over as if somebody was already shooting at you. Act first and think afterwards, otherwise you may not have time to act. Never leave your formation on any account—you'll never get back into it if you do, unless it's your lucky day; the sky is full of Huns waiting to pile up their scores and it's people like you that make it possible. Keep your eyes peeled and never stop looking for one instant. Watch the sun and never fly straight for more than two minutes at a time if you can't see what's up in the sun. Turn suddenly as if you've seen something—and you may see something. Never mind archie—it never hits anything. Watch out for balloon cables if you have to come home under 5,000. If a Hun gets on your tail, don't try to get away. Go for him. Try and bite him as if you were a mad dog; try and ram him—he'll get out of your way then. Never turn if you are meeting a Hun head-on; it isn't done. Don't shoot outside 200 feet—it's a waste of ammunition. Keep away from clouds, and, finally, keep away from balloons. It's suicide. If you want to commit suicide, do it here, because then someone else can have your bus. If you see anything you don't understand, let it alone; never let your curiosity get the better of you. If I wave my hand above my head—make for home. That means everybody for himself. That's all. Can you remember that?"

"I think so."

"Right. Then let's go and have a look at the Line and I'll show you the landmarks. If I shake my wings it means a Hun—I may go for it. If I do, you stay upstairs and watch me. If anything goes wrong—go straight home. When in doubt—go home, that's the motto. Get that?"

"Yes, sir."

They took off together and circled over the aerodrome, climbing steadily for height; when his altimeter showed 6,000 feet Biggles headed for the Line. It was not an ideal day for observation. Great masses of detached cumulus cloud were sailing majestically eastward and through these Biggles threaded his way, the other Camel in close attendance. Sometimes through the clouds they could see the ground, and from time to time Biggles pointed out salient landmarks—a chalk-pit—stream—or wood. Gradually the recognisable features became fewer until they were lost in a scene of appalling desolation, criss-crossed with a network of fine lines scarred by pools of stagnant water.

Biggles beckoned the other Camel nearer and jabbed downwards. Explanation was unnecessary. They were looking down at No Man's Land. Suddenly Biggles rocked his wings violently and pointed, and without further warning shot across the nose of the other Camel and dived steeply into a cloud. He pulled out underneath and looked around quickly, but of his companion there was no sign. He circled the cloud, climbing swiftly, and looking anxiously to right and left, choked back a furious curse as his eye fell on what he sought. Far away, almost out of sight in the enemy sky, were five straight-winged machines; hard on their heels was a lone machine with a straight top wing and lower wings set at a dihedral angle—the Camel.

"The crazy fool!" ground out Biggles, as he set off in pursuit; but even as he watched, the six machines disappeared into a cloud and were lost to view. "I should say that's the last anyone will see of Algernon Montgomery," muttered Biggles, philosophically, as he climbed higher, scanning the sky in the direction taken by the machines, but the clouds closed up and hid the earth from view, leaving the lone Camel the sole occupant of the sky. "Well, I might as well go home and write that letter to his mother, as Mahoney said," mused the pilot. "Poor little devil! After all I told him, too. Well—!" He turned south-west and headed for home, flying by the unfailing instinct some pilots seem to possess.

Major Mullen, MacLaren and Mahoney were standing on the tarmac when he landed. "Where's the new man, Biggles?" said Major Mullen quickly.

"He's gone," said Biggles slowly as he took off his helmet. "I couldn't help it, God knows. I told the young fool to stick to me like glue. We were just over the Line when I spotted the shadows of five Fokkers on the clouds; I gave him the tip and went into the cloud, expecting him to follow me. When I came out he wasn't there. I went back and was just in time to see him disappearing into Hunland on the tails of the five Fokkers. I spent some time looking for him, but I couldn't find him. Could you believe that a—bah!—it's no use talking about it. I'm going for a dr— hark!" The hum of a rotary engine rapidly approaching sent all eyes quickly upwards.

"Here he comes," said Biggles frostily. "Leave this to me, please, sir. I've something to say to him."

The Camel landed and taxied in. The pilot jumped out and, with a cheerful wave of greeting, joined Biggles on the tarmac.

"I've—"

"Never mind that," cut in Biggles curtly, "where the hell do you think you've been?"

"I saw the Huns—I was aching to have a crack at them—so I went after them."

"Didn't I tell you to stay with me?"

"Yes, but—"

"Never mind 'but', you do what you're damn well told or I'll knock hell out of you. Who do you think you are—Billy Bishop or Micky Mannock, perhaps?" sneered Biggles.

"The Huns were bolting—"

"Bolting be damned; they hadn't even seen you. If they had you wouldn't be here now. Those green and white stripes belong to von Kirtner's circus. They're killers—every one of 'em. You poor boob."

"I got one of them."

"You what?"

"I shot one down. I don't think he even saw me, though. I got all tangled up in a cloud, and when I came out and looked up his wheels were nearly on my head. I pulled my stick back and let drive right into the bottom of his cockpit. He went down. I saw the smoke against the clouds."

Biggles subjected the speaker to a searching scrutiny.

"Where did you read that tale?" he asked slowly.

"I didn't read it, sir," said the new pilot, flushing. "It was near a big, queer-shaped wood. I think I must have been frightfully lucky."

"Lucky!" ejaculated Biggles sarcastically. "Lucky! Ha, ha! Lucky! You don't know how lucky you are. Now listen. If ever you leave me again I'll put you under close arrest as soon as your feet are on the ground. Whatever happens, you stick to me. I've other things to do besides write letters of condolence to your mother. All right, wash out for today."

Biggles sought Major Mullen and the other Flight-Commander in the squadron office. "That kid got a Hun or else he's the biggest liar on earth."

"The liar sounds most likely to me," observed MacLaren.

"Oh, I don't know; it has been done," broke in Major Mullen, "but it does sound a bit unlikely, I'll admit."

The new pilot entered to make out his report, and Biggles and MacLaren sauntered to the sheds. "Wait a minute," said Biggles suddenly. He swung himself into the cockpit of the Camel which had been flown by the new pilot. "Well, he's used his guns anyway," he said slowly, as he climbed out again. "I'll take him on the dawn patrol with Healy in the morning. He's not safe alone."

Biggles, leading the other Camels, high in the early morning sky, pursed his lips into a soundless whistle as his eyes fell on a charred wreck at the corner of Mossyface Wood.

"So he got him all right," he muttered; "the kid was right. Well, I'm damned!"

A group of moving specks appeared in the distance. He watched them closely for a moment, then he rocked his wings and com-

"If ever you leave me again I'll put you under close arrest as soon as your feet are on the ground"

menced a slow turn, pointing as he did so to the enemy machines which were coming rapidly towards them. He warmed his guns, stiffened a little in his seat, and glanced to left and right to make sure that the other two Camels were in place. He saw a flash of green and white on the enemy machines as they swung round for the attack, and he unconsciously half-glanced at the new pilot.

"You'll have the dog-fight you were aching for yesterday," was his unspoken thought.

The Fokkers, six of them, were slightly above, coming straight on. Biggles lifted his nose slightly, took the leader in his sights, and waited. At 200 feet, still holding the Camel head-on to the other machines, he pressed his triggers. He saw the darting, jabbing flame of the other's guns, but did not swerve an inch. Metal spanged on metal near his face, the machine vibrated, and an unseen hand plucked at his sleeve. He clenched his teeth and held his fire. He had a swift impression of two wheels almost grazing his top plane as the first Fokker zoomed.

Out of the corner of his eye he saw Healy's tracer pouring into the Fokker at his right, and a trail of black smoke burst from the engine. Neither machine moved an inch. There was a crash which he could hear above the roar of his own engine as the Camel and the Fokker met head-on. A sheet of flame leapt upwards.

"Healy's gone—that's five to two now—not so good."

He did a lightning right-hand turn. Where was Algernon? There he was, still in position at his wing-tip. The Huns had also turned and were coming back at them.

"Bad show for a kid," thought Biggles, and on the spur of the moment waved his left hand above his head. The pilot of the other Camel was looking at him but made no move.

"The fool, why doesn't he go home," Biggles muttered, as he took the nearest Fokker in his sights again and opened fire. The Hun turned and he turned behind it, and the next second all seven machines were in a complete circle. Out of the corner of his eye Biggles saw the other Camel on the opposite side of the circle on the tail of a Hun.

"Why doesn't he shoot?" Biggles cursed blindly.

He pulled the stick back into his right side and shot into the circle, raking the Fokker that had opened fire on the other Camel. It zoomed suddenly, and as Biggles shot past the new pilot he waved wildly.

He saw Algernon make a turn and dive for the Line. A Fokker was on his tail instantly and Biggles raked it until it had to turn and face him. He half-rolled as a stream of lead zipped a strip of fabric from the centre section and went into a steep bank again to look at the situation.

He was alone, and there were still four Fokkers. For perhaps a minute each machine held its place in the circle, and then the Fokkers began to climb above him. Biggles knew that he was in an almost hopeless position, and he glanced around for a cloud to make a quick dash for cover, but from horizon to horizon the sky was an unbroken stretch of blue. The circle tightened as each machine strove to close in. The highest Fokker turned suddenly and dived on him, guns spitting two pencil lines of tracer. Biggles crouched a little lower in the cockpit. Two more of the Fokkers were turning on him now, and he knew that it was only a question of time before a bullet got him or his engine in a vital part.

Already the Camel was beginning to show signs of the conflict. "God! what's that?" Biggles almost stalled as another Camel shot into the circle. It did not turn as the others, but rushed across the diameter, straight at a Fokker which jerked up in a wild zoom to avoid collision. The Camel flashed round—not in the direction of the circle, but against it, and Biggles stared open-eyed with horror as the other Fokkers shot out at a tangent to avoid disaster.

"My God! what's he doing?" he muttered as he flung his own machine on its side to pass the other Camel. He picked out a Fokker and blazed at it. Where were the others? They seemed to be scattered all over the sky. The other Camel was circling above him. "We'll get out of this while the going's good," he muttered grimly, and waved his hand to the other pilot. Together they turned and dived for the Line.

Biggles landed first and leant against the side of his machine to await the new pilot. For a moment he looked at him without speaking.

"Listen, laddie," he said, when the other had joined him, "you mustn't do that sort of thing. You'll give me nightmares. You acted like a madman."

"Sorry, but you told me to go for 'em like a mad dog. I thought that's what I did."

Biggles looked at the speaker earnestly. "Yes," he grinned, "that's just what you did; but why didn't you do some shooting? I never saw your tracer once."

"I couldn't."

"Couldn't?"

"No—my gun jammed."

"When?"

"It jammed badly with a bulged cartridge in that first go, and I couldn't clear it."

Biggles raised his hand to his forehead. "Do you mean to say you came back into that hell of a dog-fight with a jammed gun?" he said slowly.

"Yes. You said stick with you."

Biggles held out his hand. "You'll do, kid," he said; "and you can call me Biggles."

Spads and Spandaus

Biggles looked up from his self-appointed task of filling a machine-gun belt as the distant hum of an aero engine reached his ears; an S.E.5, flying low, was making for the aerodrome. The Flight-Commander watched it fixedly, a frown deepening between his eyes. He sprang to his feet, the loose rounds of ammunition falling in all directions.

"Stand by for a crash!" he snapped at the duty ambulance driver. "Grab a Pyrene, everybody," he called, "that fellow's hit; he's going to crash!"

He caught his breath as the S.E. made a sickening flat turn, but breathed a sigh of relief as it flattened out and landed clumsily. The visiting pilot taxied to the tarmac and pushed up his goggles to disclose the pale but smiling face of Wilkinson, of 287 Squadron.

"You hit, Wilks?" called Biggles anxiously.

"No."

Biggles grinned his relief and cast a quick, critical glance at the machine. The fabric of the wings was ripped in a dozen places; an interplane strut was shattered and the tail-unit was as full of holes as the rose of a watering-can.

"Have you got a plague of rats or something over at your place?" he inquired, pointing at the holes. "You want to get some cats."

"The rats that did that have red noses, and it'll take more than cats to catch 'em," said Wilkinson meaningly, climbing stiffly out of the cockpit.

"Thinking of buying it?" said a voice at his elbow

"Red noses, did you say?" said Biggles, the smile fading from his face. "You mean——"

"The Richthofen crowd have moved down, that's what I mean," replied Wilkinson soberly. "I've lost Browne and Chadwicke, although I believe Browne managed to get down just over our side of the Line. There must have been over twenty Huns in the bunch we ran into."

"What were they flying?"

"Albatrosses. I counted sixteen crashes on the ground between Le Cateau and here, theirs and ours. There's an R.E.8 on its nose between the Lines. There's a Camel and an Albatross piled up together in the Hun front-line trench. What are we going to do about it?"

"Pray for dud weather, and pray hard," said Biggles grimly. "See any Camels on your way?"

Wilkinson nodded. "I saw three near Mossyface Wood."

"That'd be Mac; he's got Batty and a new man with him."

"Well, they'll have discovered there's a war on by now," observed Wilkinson. "Do you feel like making Fokker fodder of yourself, or what about running down to Clarmes for a drink and talk things over?"

"Suits me," replied Biggles. "I've done two patrols today and I'm tired. Come on; I'll ask the C.O. if we can have the tender."

Half an hour later they pulled up in front of the Hôtel de Ville, in Clarmes. In the courtyard stood a magnificent touring car which an American staff officer had just vacated. Lost in admiration, Biggles took a step towards it.

"Thinking of buying it?" said a voice at his elbow.

Turning, Biggles beheld a captain of the American Flying Corps. "Why, are you thinking of selling it?" he asked, evenly.

As he turned and joined Wilkinson at a table, the American seated himself near them. "You boys just going to the Line?" he asked. "Because if you are I'll give you a tip or two."

Biggles eyed the speaker coldly. "Are you just going up?" he inquired.

"Sure," replied the American, "I'm commanding the 299th Pursuit Squadron. We moved in today—we shall be going over tomorrow."

"I see," said Biggles slowly, "then I'll give *you* a tip. Don't cross the Line under fifteen thousand."

The American flushed. "I wasn't asking you for advice," he snapped, "we can take care of ourselves."

Biggles finished his drink and left the room.

"That baby fancies himself a bit," observed the American to Wilkinson. "When he's heard a gun or two go off he won't be so anxious to hand out advice. Who is he?"

"His name's Bigglesworth," said Wilkinson civilly. "Officially, he's only shot down twelve Huns and five balloons, but to my certain knowledge he's got several more."

"That kid? Say, don't try that on me, brother. You've got a dozen Huns, too, I expect," jibed the American.

"Eighteen to be precise," said Wilkinson, casually tapping a cigarette.

The American paused with his drink halfway to his lips. He set the glass back on the table. "Say, do you mean that?" he asked incredulously.

Wilkinson shrugged his shoulders, but did not reply.

"What did he mean when he said not to cross the Lines under fifteen thousand?" asked the American curiously.

"I think he was going to tell you that the Richthofen circus had just moved in opposite," explained Wilkinson.

"I've heard of that lot," admitted the American. "Who are they?"

Wilkinson looked at him in surprise. "They are a big bunch of star pilots each with a string of victories to his credit. They hunt together, and are led by Manfred Richthofen, whose score stands at about sixty. With him he's got his brother, Lothar—with about thirty victories. There's Gussmann and Wolff and Weiss, all old hands at the game. There's Karjus, who has only one arm, but shoots better than most men with two. Then there's Lowenhardt, Reinhard, Udet and—but what does it matter? A man who hasn't been over the Line before, meeting that bunch, has about as much chance as a rabbit in a wild-beast show," he concluded.

"You trying to put the wind up me?"

"No. I'm just telling you why Biggles said don't cross under 15,000 feet. You may then have a chance to dive home, if you meet 'em. That's all. Well, cheerio, see you later perhaps."

"It's a damn shame," raved Biggles, as they drove back to the aerodrome. "Some of these Americans are the best stuff in the world. One or two of 'em have been out here for months with our own squadrons and the French Lafayette and Cigognes Escadrilles. Now their brass-hats have pulled 'em out and rolled 'em into their own Pursuit Squadrons. Do they put them in charge because they know the game? Do they—Hell! No. They hand 'em over to some poor boob who has done ten hours' solo in Texas or somewhere, but has got a command because his sister's in the Follies; and they've got to follow where he leads 'em. Bah! It makes me sick. You heard that poor prune just now? He'll go beetling over at five thousand just to show he knows more about it than we do. Well, he'll be pushing up the Flanders poppies by this time tomorrow night unless a miracle happens. He'll take his boys with him, that's the curse of it. Not one of 'em'll ever get back—you watch it," he concluded, bitterly.

"We can't let 'em do that," protested Wilkinson.

"What can we do?"

"I was just thinking."

"I've got it," cried Biggles. "Let them be the bait to bring the Huns down. With your S.E.'s and our Camels together we'll knock the spots off the Hun circus. How many S.E.'s can you raise?"

"Eight or nine."

"Right. You ask your C.O. and let me know tonight. I'll ask Major Mullen for all the Camels we can get in the air. That should even things up a bit; we'll be strong enough to take on anything the Huns can send against us. I'll meet you over Mossyface at six. How's that?"

"Suits me. I hope it's a fine day," yawned Wilkinson.

The show turned out to be a bigger one than Biggles anticipated. Major Mullen decided to lead the entire Squadron himself, not so much on account of the possibility of the American Squadron being massacred, as because he realised the necessity of massing his machines to meet the new menace.

Thus it came about that the morning following his conversation with Wilkinson found Biggles leading his Flight behind the C.O. On his right was 'A' Flight, led by Mahoney, and on his left 'B' Flight, with MacLaren at their head. Each Flight comprised three machines, and these, with Major Mullen's red-cowled Camel, made ten in all. Major Sharp, commanding the S.E.5 Squadron, had followed Major Mullen's example, and from time to time Biggles looked upwards and backwards to where a formation of nine tiny dots, 6,000 feet above them, showed where the S.E.'s were watching and waiting. A concerted plan of action had been decided upon, and Biggles impatiently awaited its consummation.

Where were the Americans? He asked himself the question for the tenth time; they were a long time showing up. Where was the Boche circus? Sooner or later there was bound to be a clash, and Biggles thrilled at the thought of the coming dog-fight.

It was a glorious day; not a cloud broke the serenity of the summer sky. Biggles kept his eyes downwards, knowing that the S.E.'s would prevent molestation from above. Suddenly, a row of minute moving objects caught his eye, and he stared in amazement. Then he swore. A formation of nine Spads was crossing the Line far below. "The fools; the unutterable lunatics!" he growled. "They can't be an inch higher than four thousand. They must think they own the sky, and they haven't even seen us yet. Oh, well, they'll wake up presently, or I'm no judge."

The Spad Squadron was heading out straight into enemy sky, and Biggles watched them with amused curiosity, uncertain as to whether to admire their nerve or curse their stupidity. "They must think it's easy," he commented grimly, as his lynx-eyed leader altered his course slightly to follow the Americans.

Where were the Huns? He held his hand, at arm's length, over the sun, and extending his fingers squinted through the slits between them. He could see nothing, but the glare was terrific and might have concealed a hundred machines.

"They're there, I'll bet my boots," muttered the Flight-Commander; "they are just letting those poor boobs wade right into the custard. How they must be laughing!"

Suddenly he stiffened in his seat. The Major was rocking his wings—pointing. Biggles followed his outstretched finger and caught his breath. Six brightly painted machines were going down in an almost vertical dive behind the Spads. Albatrosses! He lifted his hand high above his head, and then, in accordance with the plan, pushed the stick forward and, with Batson and Algy on either side, tore down diagonally to cut off the enemy planes. He knew that most of the Hun circus was still above, somewhere, waiting for the right moment to come down. How long would they wait before coming down, thus bringing the rest of the Camels and S.E.'s down into the mix-up with them? Not long he hoped, or he might find his hands full, for he could not count on the inexperienced Spad pilots for help.

The Spad Squadron had not altered its course, and Biggles' lip curled as he realised that even now they had not seen the storm brewing above them. Ah, they knew now! The Albatrosses were shooting, and the Spads swerved violently, like a school of minnows at the sudden presence of a pike. In a moment formation was lost as they scattered in all directions. Biggles sucked in his breath quickly as a Spad burst into flames and dropped like a stone. He was among them now; a red-bellied machine appeared through his sights and he pressed his triggers viciously, cursing a Spad that nearly collided with him.

A green Albatross came at him head-on, and, as he charged it, another with a blue-and-white checked fuselage sent a stream of tracer through his top plane. The green machine swerved and he flung the Camel round behind it; but the checked machine had followed him and he had to pull up in a wild zoom to escape the hail of lead it spat at him.

"Hell!" grunted Biggles vigorously, as his windscreen flew to

. . . an invisible cord seemed to hold the Albatross to the tail of the Hun

pieces, "this is getting too hot. My God! what a mess!"

A Spad and an Albatross, locked together, careered earthwards in a flat spin. A Camel, spinning viciously, whirled past him, and another Albatross, wrapped in a sheet of flame, flashed past his nose, the doomed pilot leaping into space even as it passed.

Biggles snatched a swift glance upwards. A swarm of Albatrosses were dropping like vultures out of the sky into the fight; he had a fleeting glimpse of other machines far above and then he turned again to the work on hand. Where were the Spads? Ah, there was one, on the tail of an Albatross. He tore after it, but the Spad pilot saw him and waved him away. Biggles grinned. "Go to it, laddie," he yelled exultantly, but a frown swept the grin from his face as a jazzed machine darted in behind the Spad and poured in a murderous stream of lead. Biggles shot down on the tail of the Hun. The Spad pilot saw his danger and twisted sideways to escape, but an invisible cord seemed to hold the Albatross to the tail of the American machine. Biggles took the jazzed machine in his sights and raked it from end to end in a long deadly burst. There was no question of missing at that range; the enemy pilot slumped forward in his seat and the machine went to pieces in the air.

The Spad suddenly stood up on its tail and sent two white pencils of tracer across Biggles' nose at something he could not see. A Hun, upside down, went past him so closely that he instinctively flinched.

"My God!" muttered Biggles, "he saved *me* that time; that evens things up."

His lips closed in a straight line; a bunch of six Albatrosses were coming at him together. Biggles fired one shot, and went as cold as ice as his gun jammed. Bullets were smashing through his machine when a cloud of S.E.'s appeared between him and the Huns, and he breathed again.

"Lord, what a dog-fight," he said again, as he looked around to see what was happening. Most of the enemy planes were in full retreat, pursued by the S.E.'s. Two Camels and two Albatrosses were still circling some distance away and four more Camels were rallying above him. Biggles saw the lone Spad flying close to him. Seven or eight crashed machines were on the ground, two blazing furiously, but whether they were Spads or Camels he couldn't tell.

He pushed up his goggles and beckoned to the Spad pilot, whom he now recognized as his acquaintance of the previous day, to come closer.

The American waved gaily, and together they started after the Camels, led by Major Mullen's red cowling, now heading for the Line.

Biggles landed with the Spad still beside him; he mopped the burnt castor-oil off his face and walked across to meet the pilot. The American held out his hand. "I just dropped in to shake hands," he said. "Now I must be getting back to our field to see how many of the outfit got home. I'd like to know you better; maybe you'll give me a tip or two."

"I can't tell you much after what you've seen today," laughed Biggles, turning to wave to an S.E.5, which had swung low over them, and then proceeded on its way.

"Who's that?" asked the American.

"That's Wilks, the big stiff you saw with me yesterday," replied Biggles. "He's a good scout. He'll be at the Hôtel de Ville tonight for certain; so shall I. Do you feel like coming along to tear a chop and knock a bottle or two back?"

"Sure," agreed the Spad pilot enthusiastically.

The Carrier

Biggles sat shivering in the tiny cockpit of his Camel at rather less than 1,000 feet above the Allied reserve trenches. It was a bitterly cold afternoon; the icy edge of the February wind whipped round his face and pierced the thick padding of his Sidcot suit as he tried to snuggle lower in his "office".

The little salient on his right was being slowly pinched out by a detachment of infantry; to Biggles it seemed immaterial whether the Line was straightened out or not, a few hundred yards one way or the other was neither here nor there, he opined. He was to change his mind before the day was out. Looking down, he could see the infantry struggling through the mud from shell-hole to shell-hole, as inch by inch they drove the enemy back.

Squadron orders for the day had been to help them in every possible way by strafing back areas with machine-gun fire and 20-lb. Cooper bombs to prevent the enemy from bringing up reinforcements. He had been at it all morning, and as he climbed into his cockpit for the afternoon "show" he anticipated another miserable two hours watching mud-coated men and lumbering tanks crossing No Man's Land, as he dodged to and fro through a venomous fire from small-arms, field-guns and archie batteries.

He was flying a zig-zag course behind the British Lines, keeping a watchful eye open for the movements of enemy troops, although the smoke of the barrage, laid down to protect the advancing troops, made the ground difficult to see. It also served to some extent to conceal him from the enemy gunners. From time to time he darted across the line of smoke and raked the German front line with bullets from his twin Vickers guns. It was a highly dangerous, and, to Biggles, an unprofitable pursuit; he derived no sense of victory from the performance, and the increasing number of holes in his wings annoyed him intensely. "I'll have one of those damned holes in *me* in a minute," he grumbled.

Crash! Something had hit the machine and splashed against his face, smothering his goggles with a sticky substance.

"What the hell has happened now?" he muttered, snatching off the goggles. His first thought was that an oil lead had been cut by a piece of shell, and he instinctively throttled back and headed the Camel, nose down, further behind his own Lines.

He wiped his hand across his face and gave a cry of dismay as it came away covered in blood. "My God! I'm hit," he groaned, and looked anxiously below for a suitable landing-ground. He had little time in which to choose, but fortunately there were many large fields handy, and a few seconds later the machine had run to a standstill in one of them. He stood erect in the cockpit and felt himself all over, looking for the source of the gore. His eye caught sight of a cluster of feathers stuck on the centre section bracing wires, and he sank down limply, grinning sheepishly.

"Holy mackerel," he muttered, "a bird! So that was it." Closer investigation revealed more feathers, and finally he found a mangled mass of blood and feathers on the floor of the cockpit. "The propeller must have caught it and chucked what was left of it back through the centre-section into my face," he mused. "Looks like a pigeon. Oh, well!"

He made to throw it overboard, when something caught his eye. It was a tiny tube attached to the bird's leg.

"A carrier pigeon, eh?" He whistled. "I wonder if it is one of ours or a Boche?"

He knew, of course, that carrier pigeons were used extensively by both sides, but particularly by the Allies for the purpose of conveying messages from spies within the occupied territory.

"Holy mackerel," he muttered, "a bird!"

Sitting on the "hump" of his Camel, he removed the capsule and extracted a small flimsy piece of paper. One glance at the jumbled lines of letters and numbers was sufficient to show him that the message was in code.

"I'd better get this to Intelligence right away," he thought, and looked up to see an officer and several Tommies regarding him curiously from the hedge.

"Are you all right?" called the officer.

"Yes," replied Biggles, "do you know if there is a field-telephone anywhere near?"

"There's one at Divisional Headquarters—the farmhouse at the end of the road," was the answer.

"Can I get through to 91st Wing from there?"

"I don't know."

"All right, many thanks," called Biggles. "I'll go and find out. Will you keep an eye on my machine? Thanks."

Five minutes later he was speaking to Colonel Raymond at Wing Headquarters, and after explaining what had happened, at the Colonel's invitation read out the message letter by letter. "Shall I hold on?" asked Biggles at the end.

"No, ring off, but don't go away. I'll call you in a minute or two," said the Colonel crisply.

Five minutes passed quickly as Biggles warmed himself by the office fire, and then the phone bell rang shrilly.

"For you, sir," said the orderly, handing him the instrument.

"Is that you, Bigglesworth?" came the Colonel's voice.

"Yes, sir."

"All right, we shan't want you again."

"Hope I brought you good news," said Biggles, preparing to ring off.

"No, you brought bad news. The message is from one of our fellows over the other side. The machine that went to fetch him last night force-landed and killed the pilot. That's all."

"But what about the sp— man?" asked Biggles, aghast.

"I'm afraid he is in a bad case, poor devil. He says he is on the north side of Lagnicourt Wood. The Huns have got a cordon of troops all round him and are hunting him down with dogs. He's heard them."

"My God, how awful!"

"Well, we can't help him; he knows that. It will be dark in an hour and we daren't risk a night landing without looking over the ground. They'll have got him by tomorrow. Well, thanks for the prompt way you got the message to us. By the way, your M.C. is through; it will be in orders tonight. Goodbye." There was a click as the Colonel rang off.

Biggles sat with the receiver in his hand. He was not thinking about the decoration the Colonel had just mentioned. He was visualizing a different scene from the one that would be enacted in the mess that night when his name appeared in orders on the notice-board. In his mind's eye he saw a cold, bleak landscape of leafless trees through which crawled an unkempt, mud-stained, hunted figure, looking upwards to the sky for the help that would never come. He saw a posse of hard-faced grey-coated Prussians holding the straining hounds on a leash, drawing ever nearer to the fugitive. He saw a grim, blank wall against which stood a blind-folded man—the man who had fought the war his own way, without hope of honour, and had lost.

Biggles, after two years of war, had little of the milk of human kindness left in his being, but the scene brought a lump into his throat. "So they'd leave him there, eh?" he thought. "That's Intelligence, is it? No, by God," he groaned out aloud through clenched teeth, and slammed the receiver down with a crash.

"What's that, sir?" asked the startled orderly.

"Go to hell," snapped Biggles. "No, I didn't mean that. Sorry," and made for the door.

He was thinking swiftly as he hurried back to the Camel. "North edge of Lagnicourt Wood, the Colonel said; it's damn nearly a mile long. I wonder if he'd spot me if I got down. He'd have to come back on the wing—it's the only way, but even that's a better chance than the firing party'll give him. We'll try it, anyway, it isn't more than seven or eight miles over the Line."

Within five minutes he was in the air heading for the wood, and ten minutes later, after being badly archied, he was circling over it at 5,000 feet.

"They haven't got him yet, anyway," he muttered, for signs of the pursuit were at once apparent. Several groups of soldiers were beating the ditches at the west end of the wood and he saw hounds working along a hedge that ran diagonally into its western end. Sentries were standing at intervals on the northern and southern sides. "Well, there's one thing I can do in case all else fails. I'll lay my eggs first," he decided, thinking of the two Cooper bombs that still hung on their racks. He pushed the stick forward and went tearing down at the bushes where the hounds were working.

He did a vertical turn round the bushes at fifty feet, levelled out, and, as he saw the group just over the junction of his righthand lower plane and the fuselage, he pulled the bomb-toggle, one—two. Zooming high, he half rolled, and then came down with both Vickers guns spitting viciously. A cloud of smoke prevented him from seeing how much damage had been done by the bombs. He saw a helmeted figure raise a rifle to shoot at him, fall, pick himself up, fall again, and crawl into the undergrowth. One of the hounds was dragging itself away. Biggles pulled the Camel up, turned, and came down again, his tracer making a straight line to the centre of the now clearing smoke. Out of the corner of his eye he saw other groups hurrying towards the scene, and made a mental note that he had at least drawn attention to himself, which might give the spy a chance to make a break.

He levelled out to get his bearings. Left rudder, stick over, and he was racing low over the wood towards the northern edge. At thirty feet from the ground he tore along the side of the wood, hopping the trees and hedges in his path. There was only one field large enough for him to land in; would the spy realise that, he wondered, as he swung round in a steep climbing turn and started to glide down, "blipping" his engine as he came.

He knew that he was taking a desperate chance. A bad landing or a single well-aimed shot from a sentry when he was on the ground would settle the matter. His tail-skid dragged on the rough surface of the field; a dishevelled figure, crouching low, broke from the edge of the wood and ran for dear life towards him. Biggles kicked on rudder and taxied, tail up, to meet him, swinging round while still thirty yards away, ready for the take-off. A bullet smashed through the engine cowling; another struck the machine somewhere behind him.

"Come on!" he yelled frantically, although it was obvious that the man was doing his best. "On the wing—not that—the left one—only chance," he snapped.

The exhausted man made no answer, but flung himself at full length on the plane, close to the fuselage, and gripped the leading edge with his bare fingers.

"Catch!" cried Biggles, and flung his gauntlets on to the wing within reach of the fugitive.

Bullets were flicking up the earth about them, but they suddenly ceased, and Biggles looked up to ascertain the reason. A troop of Uhlans was coming down the field at full gallop, not a hundred yards away. Tight-lipped, Biggles thrust the throttle open and tore across the field towards them. His thumbs sought the Bowden lever of his Vickers guns and two white pencil lines of tracer connected the muzzles with the charging horsemen.

A bullet struck a strut near his face with a crash that he could hear above the noise of his engine, and he winced. Zooming high, he swung round towards the Lines.

"I've got him—I've brought it off!" hammered exultantly through his brain. "If the poor devil doesn't freeze to death and fall off I'll have him home within ten minutes." With his altimeter needle touching 4,000 feet he pulled the throttle back and leaning out of the cockpit yelled at the top of his voice, "Ten minutes!" A quick nod told him that the spy had understood.

Biggles pushed the stick forward and dived for the Line. He could feel the effect of the "drag" of the man's body, but as it counter-

Three black clouds of smoke blossomed out in front of him, and he swerved

balanced the torque of his engine to some extent it did not seriously interfere with the performance of the machine.

He glanced behind. A group of small black dots stood out boldly against the setting sun. Fokkers!

"You can't catch me, I'm home," jeered Biggles, pushing the stick further forward.

He was down to 2,000 feet now, his air-speed indicator showing 150 m.p.h.; only another two miles now, he thought with satisfaction.

Whoof! Whoof! Whoof! Three black clouds of smoke blossomed out in front of him, and he swerved. Whoof!—Spang! Something smashed against the engine with a force that made the Camel quiver. The engine raced, vibrating wildly, and then cut out dead. For a split second Biggles was stunned. Mechanically he pushed his stick forward and looked down. The German support trenches lay below.

"My God! what luck; I can't do it," he grated bitterly. "I'll be three hundred yards short."

He began a slow glide towards the Allied front Line, now in sight. At 500 feet, and fast losing height, the man on the wing twisted his head round, and the expression on his face haunted Biggles for many a day. A sudden thought struck him and an icy hand clutched at his heart.

"By heavens! I'm carrying a professed spy; they'll shoot us both."

The ground was very close now and he could see that he would strike it just behind the Boche front Line. "I should think the crash will kill us both," he muttered grimly, as he eyed the sea of shell-holes below. At five feet he flattened out for a pancake landing; the machine started to sink, slowly, and then with increasing speed. A tearing, ripping crash and the Camel closed up around him; something struck him on the head and everything went dark.

"Here, take a drink of this, young feller—it's rum," said a voice that seemed far away.

Biggles opened his eyes and looked up into the anxious face of an officer in uniform and his late passenger.

"Who are you?" he asked in a dazed voice, struggling into a sitting position and taking the proffered drink.

"Major Mackay of the Royal Scots, the fust of foot, the right of the Line and the pride of the British Army," smiled his *vis-à-vis.*

"What are you doing here—where are the Huns?"

"We drove 'em out this afternoon," said the Major, "luckily for you."

"Damn lucky for me," agreed Biggles emphatically.

Affaire de Coeur

Biggles hummed cheerfully as he cruised along in the new Camel which he had just fetched from the Aircraft Park.

"Another five minutes and I shall be home," he thought, but fate willed otherwise. The engine coughed, coughed again, and, with a final splutter, expired, leaving him with a "dead" prop. He swore softly, pushed the joystick forward, and looked quickly around for the most suitable field for the now inevitable forced landing.

To the right lay the forest of Clarmes. "Nothing doing that way," he muttered, and looked down between his left wings. Ah! there it was. Almost on the edge of the forest was a large pasture, free from obstruction. The pilot, with a confidence born of long experience, side-slipped towards it, levelled out over the hedge and made a perfect three-point landing.

He sat in the cockpit for a minute or two contemplating his position; then he yawned, pushed up his goggles and prepared to take stock of his immediate surroundings. He raised his eyebrows appreciatively as he noted the sylvan beauty of the scene around him. Above, the sun shone from a cloudless blue sky. Straight before him a low lichen-covered stone wall enclosed an orchard through which he could just perceive a dull red pantiled roof. To the right lay the forest, cool and inviting. To the left a stream meandered smoothly between a double row of willows.

"Who said there was a war on," he murmured, lighting a cigarette, and climbing up onto the "hump" of his Camel, the better to survey the enchanting scene. "Well, well, let's see if anyone is at home."

He sprang lightly to the ground, threw his leather coat across the fuselage, and strolled towards the house. An old iron gate opened into the orchard; entering, he paused for a moment, uncertain of the path.

"Are you looking for me, monsieur?" said a voice, which sounded to Biggles as musical as ice tinkling in a cocktail glass.

Turning, he beheld a vision of blonde loveliness wrapped up in blue silk, smiling at him. For a moment he stared as if he had been raised in a monastery and had never seen a woman before. He closed his eyes, shook his head, and opened them again—the vision was still there, dimpling.

"You were looking for me, perhaps?" said the girl again.

Biggles saluted like a man sleep-walking.

"Mademoiselle," he said earnestly, "I've been looking for you all my life. I didn't think I'd ever find you."

"Then why did you land here?" asked the girl.

"I landed here because my mag. shorted," explained Biggles.

"What would have happened if you had not landed when your bag shorted?" inquired the vision, curiously.

"Not bag—mag. Short for magneto, you know," replied Biggles, grinning. "Do you know, I've never even thought of doing anything but land when a mag. shorts; if I didn't, I expect that I should fall from a great altitude and collide with something substantial."

"What are you going to do now?"

"I don't know—it takes thinking about. It may be necessary for me to stay here for some time. Anyway, the War will still be on when I get back. But, pardon me, mademoiselle, if I appear impertinent; are you English? I ask because you speak English so well."

"Not quite, monsieur. My mother was English and I have been to school in England," replied the girl.

"Thank you, Miss—er—"

"Marie Janis is my name."

"Mademoiselle," he said earnestly, "I've been looking for you all my life"

"A charming name more charming even than this spot of heaven," said Biggles warmly. "Have you a telephone, Miss Janis? You see, although the matter is not urgent, if I do not ring up my Squadron to say where I am, someone may fly around to look for me," he explained.

The thought of Mahoney spotting his Camel from the air and landing did not, in the circumstances, fill him with the enthusiasm one might normally expect.

"Come and use the telephone, m'sieur le Capitaine," said the girl, leading the way. "May I offer you *un petit verre*?"

"May you?" responded Biggles, warmly. "I should say you may!"

Five hours later Biggles again took his place in the cockpit of the Camel which a party of ack-emmas had now repaired. He took off and swung low over the orchard, waving gaily to a slim blue-clad figure that looked upwards and waved back.

Rosy clouds drifted across the horizon as he made the short flight back to the aerodrome.

"That girl's what I've been reading about," he told himself. "She's the 'Spirit of the Air', and she's going to like me an awful lot if I know anything about it. Anyway, I'd be the sort of skunk who'd give rat poison to orphans if I didn't go back and thank her for her hospitality."

. . . . .

Biggles, a week later, seated on an old stone bench in the orchard, sighed contentedly. The distant flickering beam of a searchlight on the war-stricken sky meant nothing to him; the rumble of guns along the line seemed very far away. His arm rested along the back of the seat; a little head, shining whitely in the moonlight, nestled lightly on his sleeve. In the short time that had elapsed since his forced landing, he had made considerable progress.

"Tell me, Marie," he said, "do you ever hear from your father?"

"No, m'sieur," replied the girl sadly. "I told you he was on a visit to the north when war was declared. In the wild panic of the Boche advance he was left behind in what is now the occupied territory. Communication with that part of France is forbidden, but I have had two letters from him which were sent by way of England by friends. I have not even been able to tell him that maman is—dead!"

Tears shone for a moment in her eyes, and Biggles stirred uncomfortably.

"It is a hell of a war," he said compassionately.

"If only I could get a letter to him to say that maman—*est mort* and that I am looking after things until he returns, I should be happy. Poor Papa!"

"I suppose you don't even know where he is?" said Biggles sympathetically.

"But yes," answered the girl quickly, "I know where he is. He is still at our friend's château, where he was staying when the Boche came."

"Where's that?" asked Biggles in surprise.

"At Vinard, near Lille; le Château Boreau," she replied, "but he might as well be in Berlin," she concluded sadly, shrugging her shoulders.

"Good Lord!" ejaculated Biggles suddenly.

"Why did you say that, monsieur?"

"Nothing—only an idea struck me, that's all," said Biggles.

"Tell me."

"No, I'm crazy. Better forget it."

"Tell me—please."

Biggles wavered. "All right," he said. "Say 'please, Biggles,' and I'll tell you."

"Please, Beegles."

Biggles smiled at the pronunciation. "Well, if you must know," he said, "it struck me that I might act as a messenger for you."

"Beegles! How?"

"I had some crazy notion that I might be able to drop a letter from my machine," explained Biggles.

"Mon dieu!" The girl sprang to her feet in excitement, but Biggles held her arm and pulled her towards him.

For a moment she resisted, and then slipped into his arms. "Beegles—please."

. . . the door opened noiselessly and Antoine, Marie's elderly manservant, appeared

"Marie," whispered Biggles, as their lips met. Then, his heart beating faster than archie or enemy aircraft had ever caused it to beat, he suddenly pushed her aside, rose to his feet and looked at the luminous dial of his watch. "Time I was getting back to quarters," he said unsteadily.

"But, Beegles, it is not yet so late."

Biggles sat down, passed his hand over his face and then laughed. "My own mag. was nearly shorting then," he said.

They both laughed, and the spell was broken.

"Tell me, Beegles, is it possible to drop such a letter to Papa?" said the girl presently.

"I don't know," said Biggles, a trifle anxiously. "I don't know what orders are about that sort of thing, and that's a fact. There wouldn't be any harm in it, and they wouldn't know about it, anyway. You give me the letter and I'll see what I can do."

"Beegles—you—"

"Well?"

"Never mind. Come to the house and we will write the letter together."

Hand in hand they walked slowly towards the house. The girl took a writing-pad from a desk and began to write; the door opened noiselessly and Antoine, Marie's elderly manservant, appeared.

"Did you ring, mademoiselle?" he asked.

"Merci, Antoine."

"Do you know," said Biggles, after the man had withdrawn, "I don't like the look of that bloke. I never saw a nastier-looking piece of work in my life."

"But what should I do without Antoine and Lucille, his wife? They are the only two that stayed with me all the time. Antoine is a dear, he only thinks of me," said the girl reproachfully.

"I see," said Biggles. "Well, go ahead with the letter."

The girl wrote rapidly.

"Look," she smiled when it was finished. "Read it and tell me if you do not think it is a lovely letter to a long-lost father."

Biggles read the first few lines and skipped the rest, blushing. "I don't want to read your letter, kid," he said.

Marie sealed the letter, addressed it, and tied it firmly to a small paperweight. "Now," she said; "What can we use for a banner?"

"You mean a streamer," laughed Biggles.

"Yes, a streamer. Why! Here is the very thing." She took a black-and-white silk scarf from the back of a chair and tied the paperweight to it. "There you are, *mon aviateur*," she laughed. "Take care, do not hit Papa on the head or he will wish I had not written."

Biggles slipped the packet into the pocket of his British "warm" and took her in his arms impatiently.

Arriving at the aerodrome he went to his quarters and flung the coat on his bed, and then made his way across to the mess for a drink. As the door of his quarters closed behind him, two men—an officer in uniform and a civilian—entered the room. Without a moment's hesitation the civilian picked up the coat and removed the letter from the pocket.

"You know what to do," he said grimly.

"How long will you be?"

"An hour. Not more. Keep him until 11.30, to be on the safe side," said the civilian.

"I will," replied the officer, and followed Biggles into the mess.

. . . . .

Biggles, humming gaily, headed for home. His trip had proved uneventful and the dropping of Marie's letter ridiculously simple. He had found the château easily, and swooping low had seen the black-and-white scarf flutter onto the lawn. Safely back across the Line he was now congratulating himself upon the success of his mission. 287, the neighbouring S.E.5 Squadron, lay below, and it occurred to him to land and pass the time of day with them.

Conscious that many eyes would be watching him, he side-slipped in and flattened out for his most artistic landing. There was a sudden crash, the Camel swung violently and tipped up onto its nose. Swearing savagely, he climbed out and surveyed the damage.

"Why the devil don't you fellows put a flag or something on this sunken road?" he said bitterly to Wilkinson and other pilots who had hurried to the scene; and pointing to the cause of his misadventure, "Look at that mess."

"Well, most people know about that road," said Wilkinson. "If I'd have known you were coming I'd have had it filled in altogether. Never mind; it's only a tyre and the prop gone. Our fellows will have it right by tomorrow. Come and have a drink; I'll find you transport to take you home. The C.O.'s on leave, so you can use his car."

"Righto, but I'm not staying to dinner," said Biggles emphatically, "I'm on duty tonight," he added, thinking of a moonlit orchard and an old stone seat.

It was nearly eight o'clock when he left the aerodrome, seated at the wheel of the borrowed car. He had rung up Major Mullen and told him that he would be late, and now, thrilling with anticipation, he headed for the home of the girl who was making life worth living and the war worth fighting for.

The night was dark, for low clouds were drifting across the face of the moon; a row of distant archie-bursts made him look up, frowning. A bomb raid, interrupting the story of his successful trip, was the last thing he wanted. His frown deepened as the enemy aircraft and the accompanying archie drew nearer.

"They're coming right over the house, blast 'em," he said, and switching off his lights raced for the orchard. "My God! they're low!" he muttered, as he tore down the road, the roar of the engines of the heavy bombers in his ears. "They're following this road, too." He wondered where they were making for, trying to recall any possible objective on their line of flight. That he himself might be in danger did not even occur to him. He was less than five miles from the house now, and taking desperate chances to race the machines. "The poor kid'll be scared stiff if they pass over her as low as this."

With every nerve taut he tore down the road. He caught his breath suddenly. What was that? A whistling screech filled his ears and an icy hand clutched his heart. Too well he knew the sound.

"Let me go, damn you," snarled Biggles, struggling like a madman

Boom! Boom! Boom! Three vivid flashes of orange fire leapt towards the sky. Boom! Boom! Boom!—and then three more.

"My God! What are they fanning, the fools? There is only the forest there," thought Biggles, as, numb with shock, he raced round the last bend. Six more thundering detonations, seemingly a hundred yards ahead, nearly split his eardrums, but still he did not pause. He tried to think, but could not; he had lost all sense of time and reason. He seemed to have been driving for ever, and he cursed as he drove. Searchlights probed the sky on all sides and subconsciously he noticed that the noise of the engines was fading into the distance.

"They've gone," he said, trying hard to think clearly. "God! If they've hit the house!"

He jammed on his brakes with a grinding screech as two men sprang out in front of the car as he turned in the gates, but he was not looking at them. One glance showed him that the house was a blazing pile of ruins. He sprang out of the car and darted towards the conflagration, but a hand closed on his arm like a vice.

Biggles, white-faced, turned and struck out viciously. "My girl's in there, blast you," he muttered.

A sharp military voice penetrated his stunned brain. "Stand fast, Captain Bigglesworth," it said.

"Let me go, damn you," snarled Biggles, struggling like a madman.

"One more word from you, Captain Bigglesworth, and I'll put you under close arrest," said the voice, harshly.

"You'll what?" Biggles turned, his brain fighting for consciousness. "You'll what?" he cried again incredulously.

He saw the firelight gleam on the fixed bayonets of a squad of Tommies; Colonel Raymond of Wing Headquarters and another man stood near them. Biggles passed his hand over his eyes, swaying.

"I'm dreaming," he said, "that's it, dreaming. God! What a hell of a nightmare! I wish I could wake up."

"Take a drink, Bigglesworth, and pull yourself together," said

Colonel Raymond, passing him a flask.

Biggles emptied the flask and handed it back.

"I'm going now," said the Colonel. "I'll see you in the morning. This officer will tell you all you need to know," he concluded, indicating a dark-clad civilian standing near. "Good night, Biggles-worth."

"Good night, sir."

"Tell me," said Biggles, with an effort, "is she—in there?"

The man nodded.

"Then that's all I need to know," said Biggles, slowly turning away.

"I'm sorry, but there are other things you will have to know," returned the man.

"Who are you?" said Biggles curiously.

"Major Charles, of the British Intelligence Service."

"Intelligence!" repeated Biggles, the first ray of light bursting upon him.

"Come here a moment." Major Charles switched on the lights of his car. "Yesterday, a lady asked you to deliver a message for her, did she not?" he asked.

"Why—yes."

"Did you see it?"

"Yes!"

"Was this it?" said Major Charles, handing him a letter.

Biggles read the first few lines, dazed. "Yes," he said, "that was it."

"Turn it over."

Unconsciously, Biggles obeyed. He started as his eyes fell on a tangle of fine lines that showed up clearly. In the centre was a circle.

"Do you recognize that?"

"Yes."

"What is it?"

"It is a map of 266 Squadron aerodrome," replied Biggles, like a child reciting a catechism.

"You see the circle?"

"Yes."

"The officers' mess. Perhaps you understand now. The letter you were asked to carry had been previously prepared with a solution of invisible ink and contained such information that, had you delivered it, your entire squadron would have been wiped out tonight, and you as well. The girl sent you to your death, Captain Bigglesworth."

"I'll not believe it," said Biggles distinctly. "But I did deliver the letter anyway," he cried suddenly.

"Not this one," said Major Charles, smiling queerly. "You delivered the one we substituted."

"Substituted!"

"We have watched this lady for a long time. You have been under surveillance since the day you force-landed, although your record put you above suspicion."

"And on the substituted plan you marked her home to be bombed instead of the aerodrome?" sneered Biggles. "Why?"

Major Charles shrugged his shoulders. "The lady was well connected. There might have been unexpected difficulties connected with an arrest, yet her activities had to be checked. She had powerful friends in high places. Well, I must be going; no doubt you will hear from Wing in the morning."

Biggles walked a little way up the garden path. The old stone seat glowed dully crimson. "Bah!" he muttered, turning, "what a fool I am. What a hell of a war this is."

He drove slowly back to the aerodrome. On his table lay a letter. Ripping it open eagerly he read:

> Cher,
>
> I have something important to ask you—something you must do for me. Tonight at seven o'clock I will come for you. It is important. Meet me in the road by the aerodrome. I will be very kind to you, my Biggles.
>
> MARIE

Biggles, with trembling hands, sat on the bed and reread the letter, trying to reason out its purport. "She timed the raid for eight," he said to himself, "when all officers would be dining in the mess. She knew I should be there and wrote this to bring me out. She knew I'd never leave her waiting on the road—that was the way of it. She must have cared, or she wouldn't have done that. When I didn't come she went back home. She didn't even know I hadn't seen her letter—how could she? Now she's dead. If I hadn't landed at 287 I should be with her now. Well, she'll never know."

He rose wearily. Voices were singing in the distance, and he smiled bitterly as he heard the well-remembered words:

Who minds to the dust returning,
  Who shrinks from the sable shore,
Where the high and haughty yearning
  Of the soul shall be no more?

So stand by your glasses steady,
  This world is a world of lies;
A cup to the dead already,
  Hurrah! for the next man who dies.

A knock on the door aroused him from his reverie. An orderly of the guard entered.

"A lady left this for you," he said, holding out a letter.

"A lady?—When?" said Biggles, holding himself in hand with a mighty effort.

"About ten minutes ago, sir. Just before you came in. She came about eight and said she must see you, sir, but I told her you weren't here."

"Where is she now?"

"She's gone, sir, she was in a car. She told me to bring the letter straight to you when you returned, sir."

"All right—you may go."

Biggles took the letter, fighting back a wild desire to shout, opened it, and read:

“A lady left this for you,” he said, holding out a letter

Goodbye, my Biggles,

You know now. What can I say? Only this. Our destinies are not always in our own hands—always try to remember that, my Biggles. That is all I may say. I came tonight to take you away or die with you, but you were not here. And remember that one thing in this world of war and lies is true: my love for you. It may help you, as it helps me. Take care of yourself. Always I shall pray for you. If anything happens to you I shall know, but if to me, you will never know. My last thought will be of you. We shall meet again, if not in this world then in the next, so I will not say goodbye,

Au revoir,
MARIE.

"And they think she's dead," said Biggles softly. "She risked her life to tell me this."

He kissed the letter tenderly, then held it to the candle and watched it burn away.

He was crumbling the ashes between his fingers when the door opened and Mahoney entered. "Hullo, laddie, what's wrong; had a fire?" he inquired.

"Yes," replied Biggles slowly, "foolish of me; got my fingers burnt a bit, too."

The Last Show

In the days that followed his tragic *affaire*, Biggles flew with an abandon and with such utter disregard of consequences, that Major Mullen knew that if he persisted it could only be a matter of time before he "failed to return". The C.O. had not mentioned the affair of the girl to him, but Biggles knew that he must be aware of the main facts of the case, or he would certainly have asked him why he had been called to Headquarters.

However much the Major knew, he said nothing, but he watched his Flight-Commander's behaviour with deep-rooted anxiety. He called MacLaren and Mahoney into his office to discuss the matter with them.

Mahoney nodded sympathetically as he listened to the C.O.'s plaint. "Biggles is finished unless he takes a rest," he said. "He's drinking whisky for his breakfast, and you know what that means—he's going fast. He drank half a bottle of whisky yesterday morning before daylight, and he walked up to the sheds as sober as I was. A fellow doesn't get drunk when he's in the state Biggles is in. It's no use talking to him—you know that as well as I do. He's got to the stage when he takes advice as a personal affront against his flying. It's a pity, but most of us go that way at the end, I suppose. Newland, of 287, told me confidentially the other day that a blue pigeon follows him in the air wherever he goes, and he meant it."

"Well, I shall have to send him home, whether he likes it or not," went on the Major, "but it will break his heart if I don't find a good excuse. Now look, you fellows. I've got to send somebody home to form a new Squadron—of Snipes, I believe—and bring it over. You are both senior to Bigglesworth; you are both due for promotion. I shall be going to Wing in a week or two I hear, so one of you will have to take over 266. Do you mind if I send Bigglesworth home for the new Squadron?" added the C.O., looking at the two Captains apologetically.

"Not me, sir," said Mahoney instantly.

"Nor I, sir," echoed MacLaren.

"Thank you. That's what I wanted to know," said the Major. "I'll send him home, then. Where is he now?"

"He's in the air," replied Mahoney. "He's never on the ground. God knows where he goes, it must be miles over; I never see him on patrol."

The C.O. nodded. "Well, he can't get away with that much longer. They're bound to get him. By the way, there's a big show tomorrow—it will be in orders tonight. You'd better have a good look round your machines."

. . . . .

Biggles, cruising at 18,000 feet, turned in the direction of Lille without being really conscious of the fact. He surveyed the surrounding air coldly and dispassionately for signs of enemy aircraft, but except for a formation of Bristol Fighters homeward bound, far below, the sky was empty. His thoughts wandered back to the girl who had come into his life. Where was she now? Where had she gone on that tragic night of disillusionment? Had she been caught? That was the thought that made the day a torture and night a hell. He visualized her in the cold-grey of dawn with a bandage over her eyes facing a firing party in some gloomy French prison.

A volley of shots rang out, something jerked the rudder-bar from his feet and brought him back to the realities of life with a start. He half-rolled and looked around; a Hannoverian was rapidly receding into the distance. He frowned at it in surprise and consternation. "Good Lord! I must have nearly flown into it without seeing it, and the observer had a crack at me as he went by," he mused. "If it had been a D.VII—" he shrugged his shoulders. What did it matter —what did anything matter?

He looked downwards to pick up his bearings; the landscape was familiar, for he had seen it a dozen times during the past week. To his left lay Lille, the worst hot-bed of archie in the whole of France. On his right a narrow, winding road led to the village of Vinard and the Château Boreau—his only link with Marie. She might even be there now—the thought occurred to him for the first time. How could she have reached it? Spies went to and fro across the line, he reflected, nobody knew how, except the chosen few whose hazardous business it was. He looked around the sky, but could see nothing; he put the stick forward and commenced to spiral down in wide circles.

At 5,000 feet he hesitated. Dare he risk losing any more height? He looped, half-rolled, came out and looped again, half-rolling off the top of it. Then he spun. He came out at 2,000 feet and studied the Château intently. No one was in sight—yes—his eye caught a movement at the end of the garden and he glided lower. He knew that he was taking a foolish risk, but his curiosity overcame his caution.

Someone was waving—what? He put his nose down in a swift dive and then zoomed upwards exultantly, his heart beating tumultuously. Had his eyes betrayed him or had he seen a blue-clad figure waving a black-and-white scarf? He looked back; the black-and-white scarf was spread on the lawn. He turned the Camel in the direction of the Lines and raced for home, his mind in a whirl.

"I'm mad," he grated between his clenched teeth. "She must be a spy or she wouldn't be there." The thought seemed to chill him, and only then did he realize that he still hoped that the authorities were mistaken in their belief that she was engaged in espionage.

Doubts began to assail him. Had he really seen her—or had it been a trick of the imagination? It might have been someone else; he was too far away to recognize features.

"She's a spy, anyway. I must be stark, staring mad," he told himself, as he dodged and twisted away from a close salvo of archie.

Half-way home he had the good fortune to fall in with a

Biggles forced his way to the front rank of the group

formation of S.E.5's, to which he attached himself. Safely over the Lines he waved them farewell and was soon back at Maranique. He made his way to the mess and thrust himself into a group of officers clustered around the noticeboard.

"What's on, chaps?" he asked.

"Big show tomorrow, Biggles," replied Mahoney.

"What is it?"

"Escort—a double dose. Eighteen 'Nines' are bombing Aerodrome 27 in the morning and the same lot are doing an objective near Lille in the afternoon. We and 287 are escorting. 287 are up in the gallery, and we're sticking with the formation. Rendezvous over Mossyface at 10,000 feet at ten ack-emma."

"Good God! Have they discovered the German Headquarters Staff or something?"

"Shouldn't be surprised. Must be something important to do the two shows. The Aerodrome 27 show was on first—and the second show came through later. They must be going to try and blot something off the map; the idea's all right if the bombers could only hit the thing."

Biggles nodded moodily, for the show left him unmoved. Escort was boring business, particularly in his present state of mind. Later in the evening another notice was put on the board which was greeted with loud cheers. Biggles forced his way to the front rank of the group and read:

Promotions

Act. Capt. J. Bigglesworth, M.C., to Major W.E.F.
10.11.18. (Authority) P. 243/117/18.

Postings

Major J. Bigglesworth, from 266 Squadron to Command 319
Squadron.
H.E., W.E.F. 11.11.18 P. 243/118/18.

Biggles looked at the notice unbelievingly. He turned to Major Mullen, who had just entered.

"So I'm going home, sir," he said in a strained voice.

"Yes, Bigglesworth. Wing wants you to fetch 319 out. I believe you're getting Snipes—you'll be able to make rings round our Camels."

"Camels are good enough for me," protested Biggles. "That's the trouble with this damn war; people are never satisfied. Let us stick to Camels and S.E.'s and let the Boche have their D.Sevens—damn all this chopping and changing about. I've heard a rumour about a new kite called a Salamander that carries a sheet of armour plate. Why! I'll tell you. Some brass-hat's got hit in the pants and that's the result. What with sheet iron, oxygen to blow your guts out, and electrically heated clothing to set fire to your kidneys, this war is going to bits."

"You'll talk differently when you get your Snipes," laughed the Major.

"Orders say I'm to move off tomorrow."

"Yes, that's right."

"Good. You can give my love to the Huns at Aerodrome 27 and —what's the name of the other target they're going to fan down?"

"Oh, it's a new one to me," replied the Major. "Place near Lille, Château Boreau or something like that—cheerio—see you later."

It was as well that he did not pause to take a second glance at his Flight-Commander's face, or he might have asked awkward questions. For a full minute Biggles remained rooted to the spot with the words ringing in his ears.

"Château Boreau, eh?" he said, under his breath. "So they know about that. My God! How the devil did those nosy-parkers on Intelligence find that out?" he muttered bitterly.

Mahoney slapped him on the back. "Have a drink, Biggles," he cried.

Biggles swung round with a curse. "No, I didn't mean that, old lad," he said quickly. "I was a bit upset at leaving the Squadron. Sorry—what are you having, everybody?" he called aloud. "Drinks are on me tonight."

Dinner was a boisterous affair; the usual farewell speeches were made and everybody was noisily happy. Biggles, pale-faced, with his eyes gleaming unnaturally, held the board.

"So tomorrow I am doing my last show," he concluded.

The C.O. looked up quickly. "But I thought you were going in the morning," he exclaimed in surprise.

"In the afternoon, if you don't mind, sir," answered Biggles. "I must do one more show with 266."

Major Mullen nodded. "All right," he said; "but don't take any chances," he added. "I ought to pack you off in the morning, really."

Biggles spent a troubled and restless night. Why he had asked to be allowed to fly with the morning show he hardly knew, unless it was to delay departure as long as possible. He racked his brain to find an excuse to postpone it until the evening in order to learn the result of the bombing of the Château. If he was unable to do that, he had decided to ask Mac or Mahoney to try to send him copies of the photographs of the bomb-bursts.

Thinking things over, he realized that his first fears that the Château was to be bombed because Intelligence had learned that Marie had made her way there, were unfounded. It was far more likely that they had known for some time that the building housed certain members of the German Headquarters or Intelligence Staff, and the recent trouble had simply served to expedite their decision to bomb it.

What could he do about it? Nothing, he decided despairingly, absolutely nothing. It crossed his mind that he might drop a message of warning, but he dismissed the thought at once, because such an act would definitely make him a traitor to his own side. The thought of returning to England and leaving the girl to her fate without lifting a finger to save her nearly drove him to distraction. After all, the girl had tried to save him when the position had been reversed!

He was glad when his batman brought him his early morning tea, and he arose, weary and hollow-eyed. Ten o'clock found him in the air heading for the Line and the Boche aerodrome at Lille. Behind him were Cowley and Algy Lacey. On his left were the bombers, the sun flashing on their varnished wings, the observers leaning

He looked up again just in time to see the leader fire a green Very light

carelessly on their Scarff rings. Beyond was Mahoney and 'A' Flight. Somewhere in the rear was MacLaren and 'B' Flight, while two thousand feet above he could see the S.E.5's.

"What a sight," thought Biggles, as his eyes swept over the thirty-six machines; "it will take a Hun with some nerve to tackle this lot."

The observer in the nearest "Nine" waved to him, crossed his fingers and pointed; Biggles, following the direction indicated, saw half-a-dozen Fokker Triplanes flying parallel with them. Presently they turned away and disappeared into the distance. The observer waved and laughed and held out his hands with the thumbs turned up.

"Yes," agreed Biggles mentally, "they spotted the S.E.'s up top. They thought better of it, and I don't wonder."

He was sorry that the Huns had departed, for he was aching for action. For three-quarters of an hour they flew steadily into enemy sky, and then the leader of the bombers, conspicuous by his streamers, began to turn.

"He's coming round into the wind," thought Biggles; "we must be over the objective."

He looked down and beheld the aerodrome. He looked up again just in time to see the leader fire a green Very light; eighteen 112-lb. bombs swung off their racks into space.

A moment later a second lot of eighteen bombs followed the first. Keeping a watchful eye on his position in the formation Biggles snatched quick glances at the earth below. What a time it seemed to take the bombs to reach the ground.

"Damn it, they can't all be duds," he muttered. "Ah, there they go."

A group of smoke-bursts appeared on the aerodrome, and, a moment later, another group.

The second lot were better than the first. One bomb had fallen directly onto a hangar, one had burst among the machines on the tarmac, and another had struck some buildings just behind. The rest of the bombs had scattered themselves over the aerodrome.

"There will have to be a lot of spade work there before anybody will try any night-landings," grinned Biggles, as he visualized the havoc the bombs had caused to the surface of the aerodrome.

The faint crackle of guns reached his ears above the noise of the engines; he looked quickly over his shoulder and caught his breath as his eyes fell on a mixed swarm of Fokker D.VII's and triplanes coming down almost vertically on the rearmost "Nines". The gunners in the back seats were crouching low behind their Lewis guns. For a brief moment, as the enemy came within range, the air was full of sparkling lines of tracer, and then the Fokkers disappeared through and below the bombers.

He saw MacLaren's machine wallow for a moment like a rolling porpoise, and then, with the rest of his Flight, plunge down in the wake of the enemy machines.

"God! There must be thirty of them, and they mean business, coming in like that," thought Biggles, as he rocked his wings and roared down into the whirling medley below. A red-painted machine crossed his sights and he pressed his triggers, but had to jerk round in a steep bank to avoid colliding with the first of the S.E.'s which were coming down from above. He glanced around swiftly. The air about him was full of machines, diving, zooming and circling; the bombers had held on their course and were already a mile away.

He flung his Camel on the tail of a blue-and-white Fokker, and the same instant there was a splintering jar as something crashed through his instrument board. A burning pain paralysed his leg, and he twisted desperately to try to see his opponent. Huns were all around him shooting his machine to pieces. He pulled the joystick back into his stomach and zoomed wildly. A Fokker flashed into his sights; he saw his tracer pour straight through it; the pilot slumped forward in his seat and the nose of the machine went down in an engine stall as the withering blast of lead struck it.

Something lashed the Camel like a cat-o'-nine-tails; he felt the machine quiver, and the next moment he was spinning, fighting furiously to get the machine on an even keel. A feeling of nauseating helplessness swept over him as he realized that the Camel was not answering to the controls.

. . . there was a splintering jar as something crashed through his instrument board

Something strange seemed to be whirling on the end of his wing-tip, and he saw it was an aileron, hanging by a single wire. He kicked on the opposite rudder and the nose of the Camel came up.

"God!—if I can only keep her there," was the thought that flashed through his brain; but another burst of fire from an unseen foe tore through his centre section and he instinctively kicked out his right foot. The Camel spun again at once. He was near the ground now and he fought to get the nose of the machine up again, but something seemed to have gone wrong with his leg. He could not move it.

Biggles knew his time had come. He was going down under a hail of lead in just the same way as he had seen dozens of machines go down, as he himself had sent them down. He knew he was going to crash, but the knowledge left him unmoved. A thousand thoughts crowded into his mind in a second of time that seemed like minutes; in that brief moment he thought of a dozen things he might do as the machine struck.

The nose of the Camel half came up—slowly—and the machine stopped spinning.

The Camel was side-slipping steeply to the right now, nose down, on the very verge of another spin that would be the last. The joystick was back in his left thigh and he unfastened his belt and twisted in his seat to get his right foot on the left side of the rudder, but it had no effect. A row of poplars appeared to leap upwards to meet him; he switched off the ignition with a lightning sweep of his hand, lifted the knee of his unwounded leg to his chin, folded his arms across his face and awaited the impact.

There was a splintering, rending crash, like a great tree in a forest falling onto the undergrowth. With the horror of fire upon him he clawed his way frantically out of the tangled wreck and half-rolled and half-crawled away from it. He seemed to be moving in a ghastly nightmare from which he could not awake. He became vaguely aware of the heat of a conflagration near him; it was the Camel, blazing furiously. Strange-looking soldiers were running towards him and he tore off his blood-stained goggles and stared at them, trying to grasp what had happened and what was happening.

"I'm down," he muttered to himself in a voice which he hardly recognized as his own. "I'm down," he said again, as if the sound of the words would help him to understand.

The German soldiers were standing in a circle around him now, and he looked at them curiously. One of them stepped forward; *"Schweinhund flieger!"* he grunted, and kicked him viciously in the side.

Biggles bit his lip at the pain. The man raised his heavy boot again, but there was a suddenly authoritative word of command and he stepped back hastily. Biggles looked up to see an officer of about his own age, in a tight-fitting pale-grey uniform, regarding him compassionately. He noted the Pour-le-Mérite Order at his throat, and the Iron Cross of the First Class below.

"So you have had bad luck," he said, in English, with scarcely a trace of accent.

"Yes," replied Biggles with an effort, forcing a smile and trying to get on his feet. "And I am sorry it happened this morning."

"Why?"

"Because I particularly wanted to see a raid this afternoon," he answered.

"Yes? But there will be no raid this afternoon," replied the German, smiling.

"Why not?"

The German laughed softly. "An Armistice was signed half an hour ago—but of course you didn't know."